Flying the Coop

Also by John Sailors

*Hellacious Homeowner: The Saga of Owen Cash
Part 1, How NOT to Buy a House*

Flying the Coop

The Video Game Mystery Novel

John Sailors

Story Crest Press

Published by Story Crest Press.

Cover design by Chiao Wei Hsiang.

Visit us on the Web at www.StoryCrest.com.
Email us at info@storycrest.com.

Special thanks to Nicole L'Esperance for her excellent editing and story
comments, as well as her expert knowledge of how to grind coffee; to
Martin Printz for editing and story advice; and to Chiao Wei Hsiang for
producing the book's excellent cover.

This is a work of fiction. All characters and
names are invented and the events
are purely make-believe.

ISBN: 978-1-938688-01-0

So if Sunday you're free,
why don't you come with me,
and we'll poison the pigeons in the park ...

—Tom Lehrer

1

A glob of marinara sauce oozed down onto an open Snickers bar on Bernard's chest as he bit into his third meatball sandwich.

His oversized body lay sprawled across a lounge, facing floor-to-ceiling windows and the breathtaking ocean view beyond.

Next came a bite from a thick pastrami and cheese, that chased down by gulps from a giant Pepsi cup.

From the third story, Bernard looked out onto beach and water in three directions, framed behind by green hills to the north and south.

The Pepsi at arm's length, Bernard toasted his high school guidance counselor, the man who had insisted time and again that sitting around playing video games all day "won't get you anywhere in life."

Yet Bernard had just completed a $120 million financing for his video game startup, OffCide Studios, a chunk of which had gone directly into his personal bank account—itself already swelling with the smashing success of the OffCide title "Murder Mystery: The Case of the Cleavered Clerk."

Bernard looked out as seagulls scoured the beach for food, and in the distance a sailboat raced up the coast—a spectacular ocean view accompanied by the sound of waves washing softly ashore.

With the escrow complete on the $1.5 million, three-level oceanfront house, Bernard's real estate agent had given him the keys that afternoon, and Bernard headed straight from San Francisco to spend the weekend—discovering on arrival a delightful gas station minimart that stocked an inspirational selection of microwavable products, more varieties of potato chips than Bernard had ever witnessed in anything less prominent than a Super Safeway, and a deli counter selling freshly made sandwiches.

Two of which he was currently alternating between.

Down the way Bernard watched the scattered beachgoers: a pair of lovers at the water's edge, a man walking a dog, an elderly woman and a young girl walking hand in hand . . .

It was a dream home; Bernard would use the upper story, with its high ceiling and no internal walls, as a huge office-studio—that is, the dream bedroom he had always wanted. The lower stories he would use for all that other stuff people did, like sleeping or cooking or doing laundry.

He had tried to buy the dilapidated beach house across the street and have it torn down to give him a view from the lower floors, as well, but the Chinese couple living there refused to sell.

Bernard had brought with him the fold-out beach lounge for a bed; the sleeping bag he had been using since he was kicked out of the Boy Scouts; a Styrofoam cooler he filled with snacks, Pepsi, and chocolate milk at the minimart; and four 17-inch laptops that sat on empty cardboard boxes—one playing broadcast TV via a digital antenna, another playing an episode of "Naruto" streaming from the Internet, and the two others showing different multiplayer computer games in progress, which Bernard would turn to every seven or eight bites to play.

The sleeping bag he held tightly over his chest, not for warmth but for protection from the inevitable spills of marinara and mayonnaise—a change of clothes was not on the list of necessities he had bothered to collect on his rush to the beach.

As the sun set lower in the sky, Bernard looked at other Cliff Shores residents taking in their own dream views in their own dream homes. Up toward the cliff to the north he saw a man standing alone on the balcony of a cliffside bungalow—all wood and glass and facing the water and hills. The man appeared to be looking out to the cliffs where a lone hang glider soared above the water, challenging birds there for air supremacy.

And back to the rear, Bernard could see another man on a rooftop garden, going back and forth between two telescopes that were trained also in the direction of the cliff—each of the two men taking in his own dream view.

As the sun set lower still, the sounds of voices became fewer, the remaining beachgoers settling in to watch the sun set.

The meatball sandwich gave way to a freshly opened bag of Lay's Original potato chips and a carton of Nesquik chocolate milk—the minimart, incredibly, had Bernard's favorite brand of chocolate milk—the only brand he believed should legally be sold.

Birds floated serenely over the water; the sun dipped lower.

The Evil Iberian Emperor conquered the better part of Europe in a game on one of Bernard's laptops, while several enemies tried in vain to assassinate him on another.

The sun hit the water.

An opponent said "good night" in a chat window and signed off, causing the sun to set also on the Evil Iberian Empire.

The actual sun finally dipped below the horizon, leaving only the dimming evening light and the sound of waves splashing onto the beach.

Bernard nodded off into the night, laid out like a loaded picnic table before the wall of windows.

🐦 🐦 🐦

Morning.

The scent of early beachside air greeted Bernard's first thoughts as he lay, eyes closed, before the open windows.

The sounds along the beach added to the euphoria: seagulls squawking, a dog barking, a jogger's footsteps along the alley, an occasional pounding of a hammer . . .

Keeping his eyes closed Bernard pictured the house from the outside: white lighthouse design, outdoor stairwell, upper floor all windows . . .

Eyes still closed he now imagined the inside—also lighthouse design: white stucco, curved archways, high ceilings . . .

The surging of the waves wove together all the other sounds—birds screeching, a hammer mis-hitting a nail, the voices of children along the water . . .

This was heaven. This was why Bernard had gone into business.

More sounds: a small airplane overhead, a motorbike on a morning drive, a hammer pounding at a nail, a bird crowing . . .

And now Bernard pictured the upstairs, his dream studio, what it would look like: the U-shaped desk, giant flat-screen TVs, the pinball machine, life-sized characters from Star Wars . . .

And finally, eyes still closed, Bernard pictured his favorite part of the house: the view, unobstructed, of beach and ocean in three directions . . .

As he did so, some point very deep in his brain located the hammering, placed it in . . .

Bernard opened his eyes ever so slightly to the beauty of the morning sky, the water, the sand, the morning air, the horrid plywood structure perched directly in front of him—

He shot up to a sitting position, sending half-eaten sandwiches and snacks flying across the floor.

There, directly across the small alley, was an indescribable six-foot-tall structure made of plywood and two-by-fours, all nailed together without rhyme or reason atop the old beach house, perfectly destroying Bernard's million-dollar view.

Bernard shook his head, tried to focus, tried to understand.

"You sleep all day!?" cried out a wild-looking old Asian man straddled on top of the structure, hammer in hand, looking down with a wide toothless smile at Bernard and laughing.

Roughly thirty seconds later Bernard stood screaming at the front door of the two- (and now to some degree three-) story beach house.

"What *is* that thing?" he shouted at a girl all of about eleven or twelve, who finally answered the door. It was the girl he had seen walking with the elderly woman on the beach.

"Oh, my grandfather built it. Isn't it wonderful?" the girl asserted, too innocent to notice that Bernard's face was puffed out in a twisted red tint.

"What is it *doing* there?" Bernard insisted.

"Didn't you hear me? My grandfather built it. Isn't it great?"

"No, it *isn't* great. It isn't great at all. What did he build it *for?*"

"To raise pigeons," the little girl said, her enthusiasm waning as she began to notice the bright red glow of Bernard's face.

"What?!" Bernard demanded.

"My grandfather is going to raise pigeons. Isn't that wonderful?"

To the girl, who stood about four and a half feet tall, Bernard seemed a towering figure, his rolls of body fat tempered by his six and a half feet in height. His odd mix of clothes was equally perplexing. He wore several layers of shirts covered by a khaki photographer's vest, its numerous pockets bulging out.

"*Raise* pigeons?" Bernard demanded. "You don't *raise* pigeons. You *catch* pigeons, you *shoo* pigeons away from your statues, you *poison pigeons in the park*—but you don't *raise* pigeons."

The girl now gave in to fright. "Well, *my grandfather's* going to *raise* them. So there!" she asserted and slammed the door in Bernard's face.

🐦 🐦 🐦

By Monday afternoon Bernard's overpriced lawyer stood with Cliff Shores' city manager at the front door of the beach house trying to explain that the rooftop structure broke city codes and had to come down.

It would have to be removed by the end of the week, they explained, or the city would remove it at the old couple's expense. Bernard watched from his front door across the alley.

They were sorry, they insisted, but city ordinances were city ordinances.

Of course, the particular city ordinances may have been strengthened somewhat by Bernard's offering financial help for a new community center in Cliff Shores, one with a basketball court, a large swimming pool, and, very importantly, a ballroom. The city's mayor really wanted a ballroom.

But even the severest of city ordinances couldn't overcome the fact that the couple understood little or no English. The husband apparently thought the group was there to compliment him on his carpentry.

"Thank you, thank you," he said.

"It has to come down. It's dangerous!"

"Thank you, thank you," he repeated.

Finally the wife produced the young girl.

"My grandmother says, sorry—they don't speak very good English," the young girl said. "My grandparents speak Chinese."

"Can you help us interpret?" asked the lawyer, who charged way too much per hour, Bernard thought, to be translating through a twelve-year-old girl.

"I'll try."

"Tell your grandparents that the structure on the roof—that new structure—is illegal. Your grandfather has to take it down by Friday, or the city will take it down. Do you understand?"

The girl was silent for a moment, shaken. Her face lost its natural cheerfulness.

"Take it down?"

"Yes, it's illegal. You can't just build something like that on a roof in this city. It has to be taken down—immediately. Do you understand?"

Then: "Yes, I understand."

"Can you translate that?"

"I'll try," she said sadly. She turned to her grandfather and respectfully began to explain in Chinese. As she did so, the man's proud face slowly lost all color, his eyes grew long.

And Bernard's heart dropped when he saw a tear go down the girl's cheek. Children, especially crying children, were a weak spot for Bernard Walker.

The attorney meanwhile strolled across to Bernard and told him the girl was interpreting for them. Seeing this, the old man turned his sad eyes onto Bernard, realizing who was responsible for the order to remove the coop. His granddaughter eyed Bernard, too, sadly.

The wife glared over, as well, though her expression was far less sad than it was murderous.

Bernard quickly backed up and slammed the door, shutting out the glaring looks, the tears, and his lawyer, to boot.

The week that followed was simply weird.

The next day, what appeared to be relatives of the old couple began showing up. Soon there were often five or six of them at any one time, men and women, sitting in chairs outside the front door, a few of them puffing away on cigarettes.

And all eyes would be squarely on Bernard whenever he went in or out—scaring him to the point where he didn't dare use the front door.

He had discovered that by going out his back door, he could hop a short wall, crawl through a hedge, cut through the swimming area of a ritzy apartment building, and then climb a short hill to the highway above, where the beloved minimart could fulfill most of his needs.

It was a fortunate find, since Bernard quickly discovered that delivery was no longer an option. That Monday night he ordered pizza from the only pizza parlor that delivered. The kid who brought it was Asian, and when Bernard tried to tip him two dollars, he replied "I don't need *your* money."

Bernard figured the kid must have known all about the problems with the Chinese family, and he didn't dare eat the pizza. He threw it away and instead settled for frozen micro-wavable burritos, and then spent the evening playing the video game "Angels and Devils 3" while eating a gallon of ice cream.

The next day, searching the Internet he found only three other places that delivered—all of them Chinese restaurants. There was no way he was going to try them; they were likely potential pigeon customers and might be angry at the loss of a potential pigeon supply.

So the small market, called, poetically, MoMo's MiniMart was it.

Late Tuesday evening Bernard thought about cooking something real, that is, not microwavable. As a child he had often eaten five or six meals a day and his mother, having grown tired of playing short-order cook, taught Bernard to cook for himself.

Now he was ready to try one of his more-complex recipes. He took a foot-long hot dog, cut it down the center, inserted a line of cheddar cheese, and wrapped the whole thing in bacon. Next he began melting a half cube of butter in a frying pan as he took to cutting onions and jalapeño peppers and covering a hot dog bun with pepper jack.

This was the way to cook a hot dog.

But just as Bernard was about to put it on he glanced out the window—and saw through the kitchen window directly across, the old woman. She was looking down, apparently chopping something in her own kitchen.

Bernard stared on, frozen by her spooky expression.

After a moment she stopped and held up her meat cleaver to examine it, then started chopping again, only much harder.

Bernard watched, transfixed.

Again the old woman stopped and held the cleaver up in front of her, and again resumed chopping, even harder.

Then, more spookily, her eyes raised with a crazed look to meet Bernard's, and the hand with the cleaver went above her head and slammed down with a thump Bernard could hear all the way across the alley.

He jerked away, realizing as he did that the butter was burning in the frying pan and smoking up the kitchen.

He flung the pan into the sink, darted about the house, as swiftly as someone of his unruly figure could be said to dart, and secured the locks on all the doors and windows.

Finally Bernard ran upstairs, locked the stairwell door and all the windows of his studio, and quickly signed onto three different online games with other live people, two of them on video chat, so there would at least be witnesses if the crazy old woman came after him.

Again it was frozen microwavable burritos for dinner.

And Bernard slept very little that night, the image of the crazed old woman burned into his mind.

On Wednesday, the movers showed up and began carting Bernard's belongings into the house, much of it up the outside stairwell, a route that offered better clearance for larger items.

What Bernard figured was a fair sample of his neighbors' extended family sat out to watch, eyes carefully scrutinizing each item as the movers paraded it by—several large flat-screen TVs, still in boxes, a pinball machine, computers . . . This was clearly high entertainment for the group of them.

Bernard stayed indoors to avoid the stares, appearing occasionally in the upstairs window.

About noontime, he was sitting on a box and looking out, munching on cheese-flavored microwavable popcorn, when he saw two workers hauling in a life-sized C-3PO statue.

Bernard's heart dropped. He popped open the window and yelled out: "Why are you carrying it unboxed?!"

One mover yelled up, undeterred, "The damned things were too heavy to move in their boxes, especially up these stairs. So we peeled the boxes off back at the truck."

Bernard looked down frantically and shouted, "Wait!" But it was too late.

Back by the truck he saw two workers carrying a statue of a nude Padme Amidala, mother of Star Wars' Princess Leia and Luke Skywalker. And to his horror he followed the twenty yards of very entertained faces to the bottom of the stairwell, where two workers were carrying a life-sized model of a nude Princess Leia herself, a royal statue that proudly pronounced her femininity in startling anatomical detail to the amused onlookers.

Bernard turned very red.

He had ordered the costumes removed so they wouldn't be damaged, but there would be no explaining that now.

That evening—to his horror—the doorbell rang. Bernard walked warily to it, picturing the old woman armed with a meat cleaver, a crazed, murderous expression on her face.

He edged his head slowly to the peephole and peered out to see instead a sight that dazzled him.

He opened the door to find himself facing a five-foot-tall, somewhat plump Chinese girl in her mid-twenties, with puffy cheeks and thick glasses, and, oh, she was reading him the riot act.

". . . mean by using your wealth to take advantage of a *helpless* elderly gentleman . . ."

But Bernard didn't notice. There was something extraordinary about this girl that captivated him. Her thick shoulder-length hair seemed to grow so as to defy actual brushing, her nose bent in a way that was fantastically cute, and her taste in clothes would have been deemed conservative on "Little House on the Prairie."

". . . am from the NorCal Overseas Chinese Community Association, NOCCA, and I am here to advocate for your neighbor, and if you think you . . ."

Bernard stared directly at her face, taking in the sound of her voice but not hearing her words. There was something musical about her voice, even as it got louder and louder.

Only after several minutes did he notice the grandmother standing outside her door, looking on as insanely as ever, and in terror Bernard slammed the door in the girl's face and ran upstairs.

There he watched sadly as she spoke with his neighbor before getting into a green Honda and driving away.

Finally, the week came to a close. It was Friday night and Bernard was again toasting with a Pepsi—never Coke, never RC Cola—cup, knowing the wrecking crew hired by the city was due the following morning. After a long, long week, the structure was finally coming down and he was getting his view back. After that he would forget all about the strange family across the way.

Pigeons!

Bernard still slept each night on the lounge chair in his now-crowded upstairs office. He had begun unpacking and setting up the flat-screen TVs on rollers, had bothered to put clothes on Princes Leia and Padme Amidala, had even taken the packing off the pinball machine—but the result of his unpacking was a room far messier than when he had begun, with padding and cardboard left wherever it happened to fall.

It was in this mess that Bernard went to bed that ill-fated Friday night, in the same spot in front of the windows, his body stacked with sandwiches and candy bars, comfortable in the knowledge that the following day he would again be looking out to the pristine view he had bought the house for.

Pairs of lovers, scattered partiers, and others drifted to the sand to watch the sun set.

At the north end of the beach a group of kids were playing volleyball, and to the south a sizable yacht paralleled the shore. Bernard could see people standing on deck, drinks in hand.

The sun sank onto the horizon, as a crescent moon became predominant in the sky.

Bernard gulped down the last of his Pepsi, considered brushing his teeth, thought better of the idea, and drifted off to sleep to the sound of waves breaking on the shore.

Morning. Again, Bernard kept his eyes closed and drank in the smells and sounds.

The birds were back, several kinds by the sound of them. And the sound of waves and the strong smell of seawater filled the air.

Bernard imagined the view as it had been before the awful pigeon coop had been erected, forced that image into his mind, eyes still closed.

Below, a jogger's feet trampled along the beachside path, a few children could be heard playing at the water's edge. A truck was backing up, a beeping reverse signal sounding out.

The morning air delivered a pleasant chill, the fresh, cold leftovers of a marine layer fog that blew in overnight and was now losing out to the morning sun.

The truck stopped, putting on its parking brakes. That would be the construction crew, Bernard realized, letting his eyes open just slightly.

A flashing light, yes, that would be the construction crew blocking off the alley with flashing yellow lights.

Bernard opened his eyes further, just a bit further. No, these were red lights. His brain tried to place flashing red lights into the scheme of the day, failed to do so.

He tried to focus, could not come to grips, closed his eyes again, then blinked open—saw the smiling upside-down bloody corpse, thought about red flashing lights—and suddenly shot up and screamed for a good thirty seconds, eyes and mouth open in horror as he stumbled out of the lounge and to the back of the room, spreading around deli meats, potato chips, and chocolate bars as he went.

Looking down at him from directly across the alley, hanging upside down with legs draped over the top of the pigeon coop, arms dangling . . . a large, crazed-looking dead man, face covered with dried blood, stared menacingly over at Bernard with a broad mocking smile that seemed to say, "Good morning! You going to sleep all day?"

2

"I demand that you arrest the entire family immediately!" Bernard shouted at the face of a police officer, who glared back in disbelief.

It was disbelief over what he was seeing. Bernard's khaki vest was wrinkled, having been slept in, and showed a salami subway sticking out of one pocket and a capped bottle of Pepsi sticking out of another.

And the patrolman somehow looked far too docile for the job at hand.

"Now let me get this straight," the officer said in a voice so slow and light that it would have made Mr. Rogers seem aggressive. "A man was murdered and hung some twenty yards from where you slept, and you failed to hear or see a thing?" The voice grew weaker toward the end, as if to assure Bernard that he was only trying to get the facts straight, not to make any accusations.

"Yes! *He* killed him!" Bernard said, pointing at his elderly neighbor. "He did it to scare me!"

"Really?" The skinny officer stood about five foot eight and had a weak face.

"So arrest him!"

In fact the officer had no idea what to do. Standing and talking to Bernard was becoming uncomfortable, but talking to the Chinese family, getting screamed at by three or four people, most of it in Chinese—that hadn't been very pleasant either.

"They say they have no idea how the body got there."

"Well, it didn't *fly* there."

"They say *you* killed him."

"Me? Why would I . . . *How* would I . . . *You murderer!*" Bernard shouted at his neighbor. "Why haven't you arrested him yet?"

"Well, I'm just not so sure. You see, the dead man is a little . . . on the heavy side—weighs maybe two-fifty or more. Whereas the elderly gentleman that lives here is about five-eight and weighs all of about a hundred and forty pounds, I'd say. I just can't see him killing the man and hoisting the body all the way up there."

"And, what, was I supposed to have *thrown* the body across the street? I know, the wife did it. She threatened me with a meat cleaver, you know. Or they did it together. I'll bet you'll find that man was killed with a meat cleaver."

"Meat cleavers don't kill people; people kill people, heh-heh . . ." the officer joked, meeting a blank stare. "Uh, a little police humor there. Um . . . But why would the couple kill this man?"

"To scare me away, so I wouldn't make them take down that rooftop monstrosity. Arrest them!"

"A little extreme, wouldn't you say? Wouldn't it have been more thorough simply to kill you?"

"Ah, but then their motive would have been clear and they would never have gotten away with it."

"I . . . I don't know . . ."

The conversation was ended by the arrival of the construction crew, a parade of three trucks, one with a small crane lift built into the rear. One of the men walked forward to Bernard and the officer.

"We're here to take down that structure," he said. "What's going on?"

"Oh my," the officer said, looking embarrassed. "I'm Sergeant Bill Peterson with the Cliff Shores Police Department. I'm afraid there's been a murder here."

The worker suddenly looked up in horror at the body hanging above them.

"I'm afraid you won't be able to take it down today. I'm sorry you had to come down here for nothing."

"What?" Bernard demanded. "Wait!"

"In fact, it'll probably be at least a week before we finish our investigation. Or two or three."

"What? No, you can't, wait—don't you see?" Bernard pleaded. "It's what they *wanted* you to do. There's your motive right there."

"I'm sorry, but these are the facts: We have no idea who that man is, how he was killed, or how he got there. The only way to access the rooftop structure is by climbing through a small trap door on the upper floor—a door that appears to be far too small to get so massive a body through."

He continued: "The only other explanation is that the body somehow came from your upper floor, which is also unlikely . . . I'm sorry, but you don't exactly appear to be in particularly good condition athletically—"

"What?! I'll have you know I play at least thirty minutes of Wii every day!"

"Yes, all the same, sir, I'm afraid we have a lot of questions to be answered and that is going to take some time," Peterson said, trying to sound authoritative but coming off apologetic instead. "Back in 2002 we once had to keep the scene of a traffic accident untouched for three weeks until we could find Judge Perry."

"The judge had to inspect the accident scene?" the construction crew chief asked.

"No, it was the judge's car, and Judge Perry himself was nowhere to be found. He finally turned up three weeks later wandering along the beach."

Bernard finally was speechless.

🐦 🐦 🐦

Two hours later there came a knock on the outside stairwell door of Bernard's studio.

Several police officers had been climbing around on the outer stairs trying to view the body—which still hung smiling spookily over at them—from different angles. And, Bernard had little doubt, trying to decide if the body could have been put there somehow from his studio.

Bernard opened the door to find a different uniformed police officer, this one trying hard to look tough.

"Yes!" Bernard said impatiently. He wore the wrinkled vest and layers of clothes even though it was warm inside. "Have you arrested those bloody murderers yet? I demand action!"

"Funny," the officer said, "they're asking the same thing about you. I got some questions for you." This officer looked more than aggressive enough for the job. His square head, shaped with sharp angles by a crew cut, matched his wide, square shoulders. He looked like a G.I. Joe doll in a police uniform.

Bernard certainly did not like the tone of voice. He produced a wrapped pastrami on rye from a side pocket, opened a corner and took a bite. His nerves were severely shaken and he needed food.

The officer looked briefly around the studio, a mess of boxes and packing materials.

"First, I had better tell you who I am. The name's Captain Dirk Toland, County Sheriff's Department, and I'm in charge of this investigation. And what we're investigating is certainly a murder."

"You don't think!" Bernard said with a sarcastic tone, the image of the upside-down bloodied face etched in his mind.

"Yes, and we are considering everyone, including you, to be suspects."

Apparently Bernard was supposed to be frightened.

Instead, he opened a mini-bag of Doritos Late Night Cheeseburger-flavored corn chips and began chomping loudly on one.

"Would you mind not eating while I ask you some questions?"

"Not at all," Bernard said, but with his mouth full and still chewing.

"So I understand you were here all night?" Toland asked.

"That is correct."

"And you live alone here, do you?"

"Yes."

"What time did you arrive home yesterday?"

"I didn't *arrive* home yesterday," Bernard challenged.

"You didn't arrive home?" the officer asked, confused.

"I never *left* home yesterday, and so how could I have *arrived* home?"

The officer blinked. Then, "You didn't go to work?"

"I frequently work from home. Wouldn't you?" Bernard asked indicating the surroundings, which looked like the aftermath of a flood.

Toland scouted the room more carefully, for the first time noticed the life-size statues—now dressed but scantily so—of

Princes Leia and Padme Amidala, as well as the pinball machine and the large flat-screen TVs on roller stands.

"Worked at home, huh?"

"I left the house only one time yesterday—to go out to dinner."

"OK, and where did you go for dinner?" Toland asked.

"The minimart up on the highway."

"You ate dinner at a minimart?"

"Yeah. And I have to say, though I do not approve of your tone—let me recommend the Hellfire Jalapeño Hot Dogs, but don't add mustard; it kills the tangy aroma."

Toland swallowed and regarded briefly Bernard's shape.

"And at what time did you return?"

"About six-thirty."

"And can anyone substantiate these details?"

Bernard looked about, the only other faces around being those of two scantily clad but silent princesses and a dead upside-down guy who was staring in with a mocking but silent smile.

He held his hand toward the face: "He will tell you nothing different."

". . . OK, tell me about the doll with the chain negligee."

Bernard cringed. "You don't know who Princess Leia is?"

"Princess *whom?*"

"You don't know, do you? That, sir, is Leia, Princess of Alderaan and Member of the Imperial Senate. She is also the daughter of Padme Amidala."

"The daughter of who?"

"Of . . . look," Bernard said, and without thinking pointed back toward the less-naked statue of Padme Amidala, and then regretted it.

If Toland looked distressed at the sight of Leia, he was more so now.

"So you dress up statues of this . . . princess? That's kind of weird. The family across the way says it didn't have any clothes on when they were carried in."

"You do not understand. They're part of my work. I happen to be the chief executive officer of a successful video game company."

Toland raised an eyebrow. "You make pornographic video games?"

"No! I bought these statues on eBay—for quite a price, I'll have you know—and I had the packers remove the costumes to protect them before packing. The costumes themselves are worth a pretty penny. Look, here's a poster showing Leia's costume."

Toland looked over at the partially unrolled poster on Bernard's desk. It showed Princess Leia as a prisoner of Jabba the Hutt, donning an outfit that made her look very different than anyone expected of Carrie Fisher.

The square-faced officer took out a notebook and silently began scribbling. Bernard rolled his eyes at the waste of time.

The questioning continued for a while longer before Toland left, feeling far more confused—and a little sickly—than when he arrived.

🎮 🎮 🎮

The docile police officer that Bernard had yelled at earlier stood looking up at the body as he struggled to wrestle a ringing cell phone out of his pocket. One hoped he wouldn't have that much trouble producing his gun if he needed it.

"Hello, Sergeant Bill Peterson, Cliff Shores Police . . . Oh, yes sir. How's your vacation?"

His attempt at a friendly smile quickly melted away.

"Uh, yes, it's possibly the worst in the city's history . . .

"Yes, a murder. The body is hanging from this pigeon loft structure on Beach Way. Smiling. Yes sir. That's right, smiling. Well, what's spooky is the body is upside down, so it looks like the face is frowning.

"When? It was found this morning. I brought in the county police and they're definitely treating it as a murder investigation, sir. Pardon?

"We have no idea how the body got there. It's very peculiar. It's just hanging there . . . with this smile on its face.

"No, so far we have no clues, no leads, no ideas . . . Did I tell you about the smile? It was looking right down on that video game fellow across the street.

"You *do* think he might have had something to do with it? Yes, I believe it. He's a very peculiar man. Listen, any chance you're going to come back from your vacation early? No? But I've never handled a murder investigation—

"Yes sir, I'll leave it to the county. Yes sir, I'll stick to representing the image of the Cliff Shores PD, as you always say. Yes sir, yes sir."

Peterson hung up the phone and struggled to get it back into his pocket, all the while staring up *at that smile.*

🐦 🐦 🐦

Inside the beach house across the alley, county officers scoured the premises, taking pictures and collecting anything that looked like it might be evidence. The elderly couple had called the girl from the NorCal Overseas Chinese Community Association, Francine Lin, and she had come to interpret for them as the police asked round after round of senseless questions.

If there had been interest in Bernard's house, there was much more in the beach house, on top of which an inverted dead body smiled defiantly down on the people below.

The neighbors had also called a relative, who was getting ready to take the girl home temporarily to spare her from what was happening. But the police said she couldn't leave until the tall police officer, the one the grandfather said looked like a Communist military officer, had a chance to interview her.

They had waited more than an hour before Toland finally arrived.

"Is this the girl?" he asked the room in general.

An officer searching under the sofa said yes.

"Hi, young lady," Toland asked in a friendly voice, an attempt to gain her trust. "My name's Dirk. County Sheriff's Department. What's yours?"

She did not trust him.

"My name's Limei," the girl said defensively. She was thin, had shoulder-length hair and a pale, innocent-looking face. But her eyes betrayed something deeper, something more intelligent.

"Limei? That's a pretty name."

"In Chinese it means *black slimy squid*," she shot back. It didn't but she liked to say it did, just to embarrass adults who tried to be cute with her.

Toland frowned. The creep across the street had gotten under his skin and now he was having trouble talking to a twelve-year-old girl.

"OK. Now please tell me what time you went to bed last night?"

"I went to bed at exactly eleven o'clock."

"Are you sure?" he asked with the stern tone of an exhausted kindergarten teacher. "Now, how can you be sure it was eleven? I know a lot of kids think they're staying up *real* late, but actually they fall asleep at eight or nine."

Limei didn't appreciate his tone. "I *know* it was exactly eleven o'clock because I was watching a 'CSI Miami' episode about this guy who gets tortured to death and then cut into little pieces, which the murderer cooks in chili and sells in a restaurant. You should have seen all the blood. Oh, and 'CSI Miami' ends at eleven."

Toland got a sour feeling in his stomach. So much for children falling to sleep early. "You watch 'CSI Miami'?! How old are you?"

"I'm twelve. And yes. And I know I went to bed at eleven because the cops finally *caught* the woman who cut that guy up with a chain saw and flushed the extra body parts down the toilet—right at the end of the show."

Toland swallowed hard. Francine Lin did too.

"OK . . . And did you wake up at all during the night?"

"No."

"What time did you wake up this morning?"

"About eight, when all the police came. You know, if you guys were CSI Miami, you'd be out hunting for a cold-blooded killer right now, not sitting around on your fat butts harassing children."

The interview continued for a short while longer, though it did not go any better for Toland. He left with a new-found distaste for children in general.

🐦 🐦 🐦

Bernard came down from his studio when he saw the crane pull into the alley. Since the side of the cab read "Phil's Tree Service,"

Bernard guessed the Cliff Shores Police Department did not have regular opportunity to remove dead bodies from rooftop pigeon coops.

Making the matter more pathetic, Phil turned out to be the only person present who was not afraid of heights. He was, unfortunately, in no way comfortable around dead bodies, so a good deal of discussion took place before he finally was persuaded—with the promise of an extra thousand dollars—to go up in his crane and find some way of lowering the body.

Everyone watched as Phil raised himself up in the crane.

"He's missing a shoe," Phil called down. Bernard stood next to Sergeant Peterson, Cliff Shores' finest, and damned near, apparently, its only.

"What?" Peterson called up.

"He's got only one shoe on. And it's one ugly shoe, too. Bright yellow!"

Peterson produced a small notebook and began to make a note, when Captain Toland of the County Police yelled to him.

"You didn't see that yet? That, Peterson, should have been one of the first things you noticed."

Phil, meanwhile, using a trick he had learned in easing large branches down from trees, tied a rope carefully around one of the dead man's legs—carefully more than anything not to touch it.

With the constant habit of studying how things work in games, Bernard watched with fascination to see what Phil might do right or wrong. There might well be a video game in this. "Lower the Body 2" or something like that.

Bodies are not exactly the same as trees, he reflected.

Bernard spoke to Sergeant Peterson beside him as they looked up.

"So with the body down, we'll be able to get that construction crew to take the rest of the mess down tomorrow, right?"

"Oh, I'm afraid not, Mr. Walker. I'm afraid it's going to be there for quite a while. This is one case that's going to be hard to crack."

"I demand that you take that structure down as the city ordered."

"No, no . . . 'fraid not."

"I can't get his legs loose," Phil called down. "The other one seems to be caught on something."

"See if you can get to it," Toland shouted.

"No way. I wish he'd stop smiling at me."

"Forget the smile. Try to move around to the other side."

Reluctantly, Phil moved the crane car back slightly, then over to the other side. Leaning forward, he tugged at the dead man's pant leg.

"There's a nail sticking though it."

"Pull it loose," Toland said.

Phil tugged carefully, but nothing happened. He tugged harder, then outright pulled, jerking the leg loose and causing the other foot to flip forward and kick him in the head.

The kick was too much; Phil lost it. He dreaded the thought of touching a dead body; he hadn't entertained the notion of one kicking him in the head.

He moaned loudly and, in a state of panic, cranked the directional lever hard, jolting the crane about ten feet to the right, where he promptly vomited in the direction of a cursing Captain Toland below.

The sight of Toland trying to dodge the vomit held everyone's full attention, so that no one noticed that the rope was still connected to both the crane top and the victim's foot, pulling harder and harder at the body as it moved.

And a moment later the body snapped loose as if out of a slingshot and flew down, headfirst—smiling all the while—straight at Captain Toland, who barely managed to duck as it came sailing by, swinging on the rope, and crashed instead into Bernard and Sergeant Peterson, who were both too stunned at the sight of an oncoming smiling body to get out of the way.

It knocked them to the ground and landed next to Bernard, smiling. Peterson cried out and jumped up in terror as Bernard screamed at him.

Toland shouted far louder and added profanity into the mix as Phil had again begun throwing up.

And watching this, two other county officers were laughing so hard they fell to the ground.

And all the while Limei's grandfather looked on from the front door of the beach house, staring in disbelief, shaking his head back and forth at the wonders of this new land.

3

After the body was sent off to the county coroner in an ambulance, everyone at the crime scene departed as quickly as circumstances allowed. The spectacle of grown men flinging large dead bodies about, vomiting from cranes, cursing, falling onto knees laughing . . . the experience left everybody present wanting nothing more than to get away.

Bernard spent the evening in a warm bath playing video games with a wireless keyboard and stuffing himself with frozen microwavable pot stickers and mint ice cream.

The Sunday after he spent puttering about the house and trying unsuccessfully to get the image of the dead man's smile—and flying body—out of his mind.

By Monday morning he had pulled himself together enough to get his attorney on the phone making inquiries to see when the city was going to demolish the pigeon coop.

Still, he couldn't bear to look out toward the water from his studio—he couldn't separate the sight of the pigeon coop from the image of the upside-down smiling body. Why had it been smiling? Don't people tend to frown on the prospect of being brutally killed and hung upside down from a pigeon coop? Bernard asked himself this over and over.

He marveled at the mystery of it.

Who was the man? Who killed him? How? Why? Why did they hang the man on a pigeon coop, and more important, why did they hang the guy on the poor excuse for a pigeon coop that happened to be about fifteen yards away from where Bernard slept?

The next thing he did was call his office and put a hold on the new version of "Murder Mystery" that the company was working on. He couldn't face work with all of this on his mind.

Not finding the spirit to get dressed and go out, he searched on the Internet for a new source of delivery. The only thing he found was a pizza shop forty miles up the coast.

So he called a taxi instead, and after giving the driver a hundred-dollar bill at the door, persuaded the man to drive to several area fast-food restaurants that Bernard located on the Web. An hour later the driver returned with two Six-Dollar Burgers hold the ketchup from Carl's Junior; two large orders of french fries from McDonald's; a ten-piece order of chicken strips from Popeyes Louisiana Kitchen, half spicy and half regular; two foot-long Meatball Marinara sandwiches on Italian Herbs and Cheese Bread with green peppers, onions, and jalapeños from Subway; and two large milk shakes, one chocolate and one strawberry, from a little ice cream shop Bernard found a listing for.

And with that he sat down to an orgy of cold fast food and video games on all five of the flat-screen TVs, which, with them on rollers, he positioned to cover any possible view of the windows and doors—and the spectacular ocean view which lay beyond.

🎮 🎮 🎮

On Sunday morning after the murder, City Manager Orland Kramer awoke at seven to a ringing telephone. The sound of a telephone at seven on a Sunday morning was disturbing, but considering the murder over the weekend, he was in no way surprised.

"Hello, Orland Kramer here."

"What's going on with this murder?" It was the mayor.

"I, uh, good morning, Ted."

"I didn't call to say good morning, Orland," the mayor said in a soft but stern tone. "What's up with this murder?"

Now, the office of mayor in Cliff Shores was not in itself overly powerful. The city was run by a city manager and overseen by a council and mayor. But this particular mayor, Mayor Edward Kennedy Dennings, gained more or less complete control over the council and the city manager when during one council session—when pretty much no one was in attendance—the group voted themselves hefty stipends for the six or eight hours they put into their offices each week, and OK'd a three-hundred-and-fifty-thousand-dollar annual salary for Kramer. Which salary of course came with a new police cruiser, a secretary, and tremendous benefits—all approved after Kramer promised to champion a new community center, one with sports facilities, a swimming pool, and, importantly, a ballroom. The mayor had insisted on the ballroom.

"Well, the body was sent to the coroner's office. As I understand it, that's about all there is to report."

"And as *I* understand it, our order to take down that rooftop shack has been put on hold."

"Yes, sir, I'm afraid so."

"Do you know what that could mean for our community center? Walker is talking about contributing a couple million dollars. We need that couple million."

"Yes, I know. But we're kind of at the mercy of the county. They're in charge of the investigation and they're getting a court order to keep the structure up indefinitely."

"What's the matter with *our* police department?"

"The Cliff Shores Police Department is really a very fine department, Ted, but they're not exactly up to murder investigations."

"Aren't we paying Chief O'Brian a hundred and eighty grand a year?"

"Uh, yes, we are." That had been passed at another of those lonely City Council sessions.

"And he can't run the first important investigation that comes along?"

"Well, actually, he's in Hawaii."

"What the hell's he doing in Hawaii when Cliff Shores has its first-ever murder investigation going on?!"

"Ron was already there, Ted. He left last Thursday. He had been planning the trip for more than a year. I've been on the phone with him. He said they'd have had to work with the county anyhow, so he's going to work remotely on the case through Sergeant Bill Peterson."

"Bill Peterson? You mean that little squirrelly guy with the squeaky voice?"

"Yeeaahh . . . that's the one. He's in charge while O'Brian's away."

"Oh God. Well, tell O'Brian to get his ass back here."

"OK."

"And in the meantime, *handle* this, Orland. Get the county to do whatever it needs to do on that roof and get it demolished. Cite safety concerns or something. Got it?"

"Yes, Ted. I'm planning to call the county here in a few minutes. I'll think of something."

The mayor hung up without saying anything more.

Orland hated this job. He had spent more than twelve years as a city manager in three cities and another fifteen in various city posts. He had suffered a career of working his butt off making cities run efficiently and on budget, and in the end it always came down to some incompetent part-time elected official stepping in with his or her own agenda and Orland would be back out on the street looking for a new job.

But this would be his last. Banking the bulk of his high salary, he was on schedule to retire in another year and a half—by which time someone might discover the city's unruly pay scale anyhow.

And then the mayor and his council cronies would be in a heap of trouble, while Orland would be spending his days deep-sea fishing down off Monterey, where he had just bought a small house at a criminally low price because of the poor housing market, and at a criminally low mortgage rate.

But Orland needed that additional year and a half of salary or he couldn't retire, couldn't keep the house.

He needed that money. He didn't need bodies turning up on roofs and police chiefs gallivanting around Hawaii.

🐾 🐾 🐾

Bill Peterson of the Cliff Shores Police Department had three files on his desk.

One was filled with notes he had prepared for a meeting with representatives of the Cliff Shores' Downtown Merchants Association, to explain the city's new parking-enforcement policy, which the merchants were up in arms about because beachgoers were taking up all the available parking spaces they needed for their businesses.

Another, which Peterson hadn't opened in more than a month, was an old complaint about people disturbing some rare birds or something such.

The other file contained documents on a murder investigation.

Bill Peterson didn't like that file.

Murders and violence and crime weren't why Bill Peterson had gotten into police work.

The first file, now that was what had inspired Bill Peterson to get into police work.

Andy Griffith, that was what had inspired Bill Peterson to become a police officer.

Murders weren't supposed to happen in a sleepy little town like Cliff Shores. The biggest crime Bill Peterson normally had to deal with was Open Container of Alcohol on the Stretch (beach).

That was why Bill Peterson had chosen to become a police officer in a city like Cliff Shores.

If he had wanted to fight violent crimes he would have chosen a city like Oakland after a lost Super Bowl, or Los Angles when CNN was running a racially charged trial live on national TV.

But Peterson had not chosen these cities. He had chosen Cliff Shores, a nice sleepy little town like Andy Griffith's Mayberry where the sheriff didn't carry a gun and the biggest challenge of the day was finding the wisdom to solve squabbles among townsfolk.

But the murder file was obviously more pressing than the downtown parking file or the file about rare birds. Bill Peterson had a two-year degree in criminal justice. He had learned little about forensics, opting instead to take courses on police equipment and department budgeting and personal law. But one thing he had learned was that a murder would be considered a more-serious case than a parking squabble or a dead bird or two, by almost any police officer.

Still, Peterson didn't want to think about it. He didn't want to think about it partially because he had no idea whatsoever how to proceed with a murder investigation and partially because the image of that large man hanging from that strange rooftop structure, with a wild upside-down smile, scared the dickens out of him.

But his boss, the police chief, was out of town and that left him as the ranking officer—well, ranking over Mike the patrol officer, Sherry the dispatcher, and old Helen, effectively the city's meter maid.

Bill thought about parking. Actually, Helen had a pretty good job. She enforced laws and never had to actually talk to anyone. Just leave them a ticket. Unfortunately she didn't get to carry a gun and handcuffs. Bill Peterson got to carry a gun and handcuffs. He was scared to hell of both of them but carrying a gun and handcuffs on his belt really made him feel important. Kind of like Andy Griffith.

The murder case was no hurry, really, he reasoned. The victim was not getting any better—or deader—and the county morgue didn't charge by the day. And it didn't seem as if the citizens of Cliff Shores were in any particular danger. It was highly improbable, Bill Peterson reckoned, that some deranged maniac with a penchant for impaling bodies on pigeon coops was creeping around the alleyways of Cliff Shores stalking his next innocent victim. No, this was some isolated crime; someone had a specific reason to do that to that man. Maybe that man had done something to deserve it.

In fact Bill Peterson reasoned it might even be a Mafia thing; it was that terrible.

The officer from the County Police was due back soon and the investigation could wait for him.

🔫 🔫 🔫

Captain Toland showed up to the County Sheriff's Department about two in the afternoon on Monday, figuring he had earned a day to sleep in after the distressful weekend.

On Saturday, once the body had been sent off, Toland returned to the station to clean up, file a report, and write up reprimands for the two county officers that had laughed when . . . well, everything happened.

They would pay sooner, if not worse, than the murderer would, Toland vowed.

He next went home, showered, and sat up half the night drinking a six-pack of light beer while watching reruns of T.J. Hooker.

Nice, solid uniformed police action, not that phony plain-clothes nonsense like the little girl talked about on CSI.

Toland felt only a pang of guilt for not doing anything further on the murder investigation on Sunday and Monday morning. After all, it was technically a city case. Handling the immediate aftermath was their problem. For his part, he had called in Saturday afternoon and prepared for a court order to keep the rooftop untouched, which meant he could goddamned well wait another day or two before dealing with it.

As he made his way across the office section of the station, another officer handed him a phone message. "Need information on Beach Way pigeon loft. Structure due for demolition. Safety hazard. Call immediately. Cliff Shores City Manager Orland Kramer."

The goddamned city has a goddamned murder and the only goddamned thing they're worried about is a goddamned bird house, Toland thought.

"I'll be damned if I'm gonna call that bastard right away," Toland said to himself as he sat down to a cup of coffee, which he intended to drink while it was still hot—and then he would begin work.

The phone rang.

"Goddamn it," Toland said under his breath.

He would have pushed the call through to voice mail, but there were other officers in the room, and he had just waltzed in at two p.m. two days after beginning a murder investigation. He couldn't be seen ignoring phone calls.

"Captain Toland here." He sounded like a tough, angry cop with an agenda—which only he knew was mainly to get at his coffee before it cooled.

"Hi, Captain Toland, this is Orland Kramer, Cliff Shores' city manager. How are you?"

"Busy, Mr. Kramer. What can I do for you?"

"Of course, I'm calling to ask about the murder investigation."

"Yes, of course."

"What do we know so far?"

"No definite picture yet," Toland said, which was true, "but we'll have one for you soon. I'll be down there tomorrow morning. Will you be in? I'd like to ask you some questions." He said this with an accusing tone, aiming to put the city manager of the little beach community ill at ease.

But Kramer had worked for more cities than Toland had visited.

"Yes, well, about the illegal rooftop structure . . . I have to reschedule the demolition crew—"

"Nope. No can do. That rooftop mess stays untouched."

"But it's structurally danger—"

"It's structurally a disgrace, is what it is. How'd somebody get away with building the thing?"

"They didn't. We were about to take it down. It's dangerous. It's condemned."

"It's a crime scene."

"You could certainly take pictures. The thing's a hazard. I have to worry about the well-being of our city's residents."

"Who might be in danger, since we could well have a murderer running around out there. *I* have to think about the well-being of your residents, too, Mr. Kramer."

"But even a slight wind could send the damned thing tumbling down on someone's head."

"So, block off the street. I think the Cliff Shores Police Department is capable of dealing with a road hazard. I left several rolls of yellow tape with Sergeant Peterson."

"Normally a crime scene can be dismantled in a day or two when a public hazard needs to be cleared," Kramer said. "I have contacts in Oakland. I could enlist help from the Oakland Police if you have your hands full, Captain."

"That won't be necessary," Toland said, now genuinely angry. "I'll see you tomorrow morning, Mr. Kramer."

And with that he hung up, feeling a surge of power at having his colleagues witness him hanging up on a city manager.

He paused briefly to admire his ability to take command of situations.

Then took a gulp of what turned out already to be *cold* coffee.

4

This is what Bernard learned from his attorney in exchange for a gargantuan legal fee: It turned out his view was not going to be restored for some time.

It turned out that small seaside towns populated primarily by wealthy elderly residents experienced very few murders and thus did not prepare tremendous resources for solving them, and it turned out that the County Sheriff's Department did not normally have comparatively more murders to deal with.

Moreover, Cliff Shores' police chief, a thirty-year veteran from large-city departments and the only city officer really competent to investigate a murder, was on vacation on Maui and was not due back until the following month.

And so the county police had obtained a court order prohibiting the city from demolishing the pigeon coop, or in any way disturbing the murder scene, until which time the case was solved.

The real murder, Bernard reckoned, had been committed on his view.

And that thought depressed Bernard more.

So for a week he did not leave the house except to make trips to the minimart. Instead of going in to work, he busied himself at finally setting up his studio—though not personally.

He brought in two technicians from his company and micro-managed their every move as they wired several high-end gaming computers and a mini supercomputer—all hooked to the three 50-inch plasma and two 50-inch LCD flat-screen TVs. The super-computer consisted of several boxes in a rack connecting several hundred processors and a series of drives. A small high-performance computing company had custom-built it for Bernard and put together test software he was experimenting with for game design.

Bernard again positioned the 50-inch screens so as to hide all sight of the pigeon coop.

And on the center screen, he continuously ran video he had shot of the view when he first looked at the house.

Along the back wall he had arranged the pinball machine, the statues of Princes Leia, Padme Amidala, and C-3PO, and a pachinko machine. These were framed by posters from science fiction films and a six-foot-tall poster of a shapely blonde in a string bikini, with long legs, richly tanned skin, and thick lips that made her look as if she were pouting despite the smile on her face.

What made the poster special was, incredibly, the girl was not real, but rather was created by computer-aided animation, a main character in "Murder Mystery," the flagship video game of Bernard's company.

And he installed in a walk-in closet a microwave oven and a full-size refrigerator-freezer, which he began stocking fuller with each trip to the minimart.

On one such trip that Wednesday he saw the young Chinese girl sitting at a table beside the market, in a spot that offered a slight ocean view and a bit of a breeze. She sat drinking a soda, immersed in a hand-held video console. Unable to contain himself Bernard walked over to look.

"What?!" he shouted when he saw the console—causing her to jump and drop it, she was so startled.

"That little console was obsolete years ago!"

"My Game Boy!" the girl cried out, a worried look on her face. She picked it up and examined it. "It's scratched. You made me drop it and it got scratched." A tear quickly appeared on her cheek.

Bernard really didn't do well with tears and kids crying and that sort of thing.

"I'm sorry. I just . . . I just couldn't believe you would be wasting your time on *that* old thing."

"I *like* my Game Boy. You're not only a murderer; you're a vandal, too."

"I'm *not* a murderer, and anyhow you should *thank* me for scratching that thing. Do you know what the video capability of more-modern consoles can do?"

"I don't have a more-modern player," the girl said angrily and took off running down the hill, leaving behind her soda—and Bernard looking for something to say.

"I said I was sorry!" he yelled. "Bring it back. I'll fix it." But she was gone.

Dumb girl, Bernard said to himself a while later as he made his own way down the hill. It's her grandfather's fault. None of this would have happened if her grandfather hadn't grown a sudden appetite for pigeons.

Bernard went back to his studio and tried to get his mind off the incident by playing a social game called "Killer Ninja Assassin Agent" on a popular social gaming site—*social* meaning his opponents were real people, not computer-generated, and he had to wonder how many of the assassins out to get him were actually his employees using aliases.

But he couldn't get his mind off the girl's crying. Finally he went to the window and watched the beach house across the street. About a half hour later, as he had expected, the grandparents came out the front door and headed to the beach for a walk, as they seemed to most afternoons.

As soon as they were out of sight, Bernard grabbed a Sony PSP and as many video games for it as he could hold and hustled down the outside stairwell to the house's front door. He rang the doorbell and waited.

After a few minutes the door opened a few inches, the chain lock barring it from moving any farther.

The girl's voice came out: "My grandparents told me never to open the door, especially for you! And I should warn you: I have a brown belt in karate!"

"Wait, wait! I brought you a new game console."

"Go away!" she persisted. "I don't want anything from you. Go!"

"Wait, no, wait! Here!" he said panicking and lightly spilled the console and games onto the ground at the door's opening. "There. It's all yours. I owe it to you. I broke your other console."

A brief silence followed before the chain was removed and the door slowly opened. The girl knelt down and picked up the console.

"This is a PSP. You're giving me *this?*"

"Yes. I have several. And these games—here, this one, it's not even on the market yet. They're all yours. You deserve to have a better game console."

"I can't take it. My grandmother would kill me."

"What? Just explain that I broke your other one. Or don't let her see it."

"I could never lie to my grandmother," the girl insisted, but the expression on her face showed that her mind was working to find some way of keeping the gift.

"Look, I have a lot of money and I want to share it. I've caused you a lot of trouble. Now I want to make up for it. But don't tell your grandmother," he said looking scared.

The girl smiled up at him. "My grandmother scares you, doesn't she?"

"Yes," Bernard said without hesitation or embarrassment. "She scares the heck out of me."

"Me too, sometimes, and Grandfather too. My name's Limei. What's yours?"

"Bernard. My name's Bernard Walker. Look, I've got to get out of here before your grandparents come back. You take all that inside and start playing. I'll bring new games up to the minimart tomorrow, same time."

"Thank you," she said quietly. "But can I ask you something honestly?"

"Sure," Bernard said. "What?"

"Why do you hate my grandfather? And did you murder that man?"

"No! I didn't murder that man. And I don't hate your grandfather. Trust me."

Limei looked down and backed into the house.

"I'm sorry for what's happened," Bernard said and turned to go.

Just as he reached his front door the girl's head appeared outside again. "Thank you," she shouted.

And with that, Bernard felt better and headed up the stairs to attempt killing a few of his employees in "Killer Ninja Assassin Agent."

🐦 🐦 🐦

From the living room window of her tiny apartment in Manhattan, Kelly Chambers could see just a tiny corner of the Empire State Building, way off in the distance—her claim to a dream home despite its being only a small corner with the rest of the view being mainly of an alley.

On this particular day, she was up late exchanging email and phone calls with West Coast executives who seemed always to forget that it was three hours later in New York.

But it had been an extraordinary week, what with the murder and all, and now George Johannsen, one of the board members, was worrying about the mental state of the company's CEO, Bernard Clyde Walker.

Kelly bit on a sausage grinder, fighting to keep the sandwich from dripping onto her laptop's keyboard. Her slim figure hid well her preoccupation with food, a liking that had nearly destroyed a number of keyboards and pieces of furniture over the years.

Kelly's small dining table doubled as a desk in the small one-bedroom flat that, even with her hefty salary, was about all she could afford in the city.

The thing was, as chief financial officer of OffCide Studios and the company's only executive on the East Coast, Kelly didn't have to stay in Manhattan, or New York City or New York state, for that matter.

She could very well move into a beachfront bungalow in the Bahamas for all the difference it would make in her work, which she carried out remotely using videoconferencing and email.

But Kelly refused to give up her beloved city, had feared she might have to move to California to take the position, but Walker, it turned out, was oddly insistent that she remain on the East Coast.

Here in New York Kelly had access to all of the things she loved—museums, world-class dining, theater, concerts, sausage grinders topped with melted mozzarella and fried onions and green peppers . . .

And she never had to drive, did not in fact own a car. She much preferred to walk most places, often covering several miles in a day—needed exercise that maintained her thin shape despite her love for food, from leading gourmet restaurants to New York's smallest delis and hot dog stands. And beyond that she could take the subway.

But over the past couple of days it was beginning to look more and more like she might have to fly out to San Francisco for a time, with everything that was going on there. First were the concerns over Walker's grasp of reality, and after that Johannsen had demanded a new audit of company finances, and that was turning up some unexplained waste.

Moreover, a review of work orders seemed to show that nothing was being done toward the company's future products, something that Johannsen, himself a major investor in OffCide Studios, was particularly concerned about.

Kelly closed her email and ran a Google Maps search on "San Francisco, Italian delis," and began taking notes. Best to prepare early, she thought.

🐾 🐾 🐾

About that same moment, though it was much earlier in the day on the Hawaiian island of Maui, Cliff Shores Police Chief Ron O'Brian lay back on a lounge chair in the shade of three palm trees, those set above a long stretch of fine white sand that led down to the ocean.

The fact that it was way too early in the day to be having a drink, especially if you were a police chief, made his banana daiquiri taste all the better.

O'Brian looked so out of place in an aloha shirt that he was instantly identifiable as a tourist. In his normal suit and tie he appeared a fierce, solid-as-rock police chief, enough character worn into his face to instill mortal fear in a jaywalker. But put in an aloha shirt on a beach lounge, what was most apparent was his wide girth and balding head.

In front of him the water was crystal clear, the waves rolled gently onto the shore, a light breeze tempered the bright sun.

O'Brian faced an ocean view that would have made Cliff Shores blush—and with daiquiri in hand, iPod playing Frank Sinatra, and a Chuck Yeager biography open on his chest.

So it was like a huge rain cloud suddenly appearing overhead when his wife showed up holding out his cell phone. There is something about wives and rain clouds, he reflected.

"This thing's been ringing again all morning," she said angrily.

"Let it ring . . ."

She set it on the table beside him. "Well, then *you* keep it. I don't want to listen to the thing. I was in the middle of a massage the last time it rang." And with that she stormed off, the rain cloud above departing as quickly as it came.

O'Brian picked up the phone and set his profile to Silent.

"Silly woman," he said to himself, sipping his daiquiri.

🎮 🎮 🎮

That Friday afternoon when Bernard walked up to MoMo's MiniMart, he again found Limei sitting on the bench. He waved to her and gestured that he'd be back after he went inside.

As he returned, Limei wondered whether it was safe to talk to him. He wasn't exactly a stranger, but he was a murder suspect. Still, she didn't see too much harm, since there were a lot of people around and she really did have a brown belt in karate.

Bernard had stuck some flash drives with video games into his pocket, and now handed them over to Limei.

But instead of Bernard interesting her with his fancy new video games, she produced the scratched old Game Boy console and put in a cartridge containing numerous Japanese games, simple and outdated, but in their cute imagination like nothing Bernard had ever seen.

And so the two spent an hour with Limei teaching Bernard new games on her old console instead of the other way around. It seemed both of them had finally found someone they could talk to in Cliff Shores.

🐾 🐾 🐾

Several more days passed, then another week, then another, and still Bernard could not think of work.

Even his engineers, the only people in the company who understood him, told Bernard he should leave the studio until the rooftop structure was down and the murder business taken care of.

Bernard refused. A man's dream video game studio is a man's castle, he figured, and he was going to stay right there and see that things were cleared up as quickly as possible—even though no one seemed to be doing anything about anything.

Bernard didn't even answer voice mail and email. Only his engineers could reach him, and that was in the virtual worlds of several Internet video games they knew he would be playing. It would take them only a matter of time to figure out which player was Bernard—usually because he stood out by beating everyone.

Then surprised virtual onlookers would see some giant combat soldier armed with automatic rifles and handfuls of grenades approaching a knight in battle armor with ray guns in each hand, and the soldier would look at the knight with death in his eyes and say something like: "You didn't answer my email."

The knight would step back, consider his options. "Sorry. I happened to have been liberating Iberia from the evil Goths."

"Yeah, well, listen, can I have next week off? I'm in a 'Guitar Hero' contest," the soldier would say.

"Very well, if you feel that *a game* is more important than *your work*."

"I do," the soldier would growl, and the two of them would launch into mortal combat, usually with Bernard winning.

And each morning and each afternoon Bernard called his lawyer, who then called the County Sheriff's Department and the city police and the city manager and the mayor, and then added hefty sums onto Bernard's legal bill, though obtaining no useful information whatsoever on the progress of the murder investigation or the removal of the rooftop structure.

And each afternoon Bernard trekked up to the highway minimart and sat on the same bench, overlooking a stretch of hill diving down to a rocky shore below. The added height offered a broad view of the horizon off toward North Cliff.

Avoiding the police and the few relatives who still occasionally showed up across the street, he took to going out his back door and climbing the short wall, where he would take a small path that wound up the hill around the ritzy condo building called the Cliffside Condos.

Then on Saturday, three weeks following the murder and four following the murder of his view, Bernard walked down along the beach to explore the far end, the north side, where he had yet to visit. He figured a taste of the beautiful area he had moved to might get his mind off the murder, off the structure, off the lost view, and off that horrible smile on the victim's face.

He walked past the few beachfront restaurants, then a small row of shops selling beach recreation items—floats, towels, bathing suits, and the lot.

A bit further down, past the few lifeguard stands, he walked to the end of a small pier. Benches along the pier were lined with men and women holding fishing poles, most with the fierce expression of hardened gamblers on their faces as they stared down onto unbiting fish below.

Bernard reflected there might well be a video game in this, mindful of how lucky he was to have gotten hooked on video games as opposed to sports fishing.

Beyond the pier, the white sand gave way to rocky terrain and a large structure that extended out onto the water.

A sign at the entrance read: "Cliff Shores Institute for Oceanic Research."

The building appeared to have a small aquarium built out into the bay, and on the far side, a narrow inlet made room to park a couple of boats and two odd-looking submarines.

A group of tourists stood near the subs watching a woman speak. She looked both pretty and intelligent, and held her audience's attention.

". . . learned more in two years than every researcher in the region had learned *ever!*" Bernard heard her say in an eloquent Indian accent. "But now, for lack of funding, we are nearly completely shut down . . ."

'No video game in this,' Bernard said to himself and walked on, curious now by the sight in the distance, ahead toward North Cliff, of several hang gliders soaring along the hillside.

As he got closer, he saw they were using a small platform on the hilltop to launch, and would go out over the water and hover. At times it looked as if they sat perfectly still in the sky, unmoving as they looked down on the beachgoers.

This would definitely make an interesting game, somehow, he thought.

He walked to his right where he saw a small snack shack and bought a hot dog, which he loaded with onions, and a large Pepsi. Sitting on a bench he looked back down the beach to the south, where off in the distance he could see the grotesque pigeon coop atop the beach house, and across from it his own house with its spoiled view.

The walk had made him feel better and the hot dog and Pepsi would make him feel more so, but Bernard wondered if he would ever get that smile out of his mind, wondered if he would ever get that damned pigeon coop down and clear his view.

5

Two days later, Monday afternoon: Bernard still refused to go in to work, but much of the same technology that made him rich meant that work could come to him—not always a welcome prospect.

He sat at his U-shaped desk, surrounded by four open laptops and the five 50-inch TVs on wheeled racks. Under the desk were two high-end gaming computers and another two sat partially disassembled off to one side, next to a stack of video cards, hard drives, and other components.

On the left-most TV screen, broadcasting from Menlo Park, was George Poston Johannsen, partner at Johannsen Twepp Capital, which had led OffCide Studios' recent funding and in the process put Johannsen on the company's board.

The next screen over showed the video image of OffCide Studios' chief financial officer, Kelly Elma Chambers, in New York; on the right-most was Chen Li, who led a software-development team in Beijing, and three of his engineers; and the screen next to that showed Lester Argyle and three other engineers in the OffCide Studios' San Francisco office.

The center screen covered up the view of the pigeon coop and the ocean beyond, and in place of the disturbing sight it continued twenty-four-seven to play the video footage that Bernard had shot of the scene—sans pigeon coop—months earlier.

On his screen, Johannsen stared sternly at Bernard, and on the others everyone stared with concern at Bernard because Bernard didn't usually react well when people stared sternly at him.

Then again, not many people had helped Bernard raise a hundred and twenty million dollars.

"I'm more than a little worried," Johannsen said, "that we have no timeline whatsoever for the release of 'Murder Mystery 2' or any other video game or product from your company. From *our* company, I should say."

Bernard bit his lower lip, wiped his hand on his face, and glared dejectedly down on a laptop in front of him, where none of the videoconference attendees could see that he had a video game going, with a would-be assassin trying to kill him in "Space Pirates of the Lost Arctic."

Somewhere in the world someone was controlling that virtual assassin, not suspecting that he or she was competing against the CEO of one of the world's leading gaming startups.

Bernard wondered briefly if George Johannsen played such games; knocking him off would make Benard feel pretty good, he thought.

"But let's talk to everyone. We'll come back to you in a minute," Johannsen said with a threatening tone and a disgusted look in his eyes.

Bernard pulled up a video control window, clicked on Effects, and made a selection. The box was replaced by a window that read, "Calibrating face," and after a moment a pink pig's nose appeared over Johannsen's nose on the left screen, replacing it and following Johannsen's head as it moved about. The nose of course appeared only on Bernard's screen; only he could see it.

"Let's get an update from our team in Beijing," Johannsen went on. "Chen Li, is it?"

"Yes, sir," Chen said.

"What's your work status there?"

"My what?"

"Your work status. What has your team been doing the past few weeks?"

"Well . . . well . . . here, everything's on schedule," Chen said, a bit of nervousness in his voice. Chen Li and his team did not work for OffCide Studios directly; they were an outsourced operation.

But they had previously spent more than two years working on pest control training websites, hating every moment of it; they loved what they were doing now, the game modeling they designed and polished.

"What does that mean—everything's on schedule?" George Johannsen replied, none too happy at the lack of articulation from

Chen, who was neither a native English speaker nor a veteran of video meetings with prominent venture capitalists.

"Well, uh . . . it means all projects are . . . current."

"And by *current* you mean . . . ?"

"Uh . . . Complete."

"Which projects?"

"Uh, the Facebook integration of 'Murder Mystery 1,' the PSP graphics upgrade to the game, and . . ."

"And what?"

" . . . And a Star Wars scene involving Princess Leia, which Bernard asked us to make for him."

Bernard blushed.

"I see. I don't even want to ask about that. But what you're saying is that your team is *not* currently working on any new products, is that correct?"

"Well, sir, every day we talk with Bernard and Mr. Argyle discussing quality, modeling, and—"

Bernard went back to the Effects window and made a second selection. This one, after the software had calibrated, put a large, royal crown on Johannsen's head, adding to the pig nose.

"But no actual work orders are pending for future products, is that correct?" Johannsen pressed Chen.

"Uh . . ."

Johannsen gave Chen a deadly stare.

Meanwhile Bernard had opened a private videoconferencing window and dialed Lester Argyle, who was on screen four. Lester was in his San Francisco cubicle, watching the meeting participants in separate windows, just as Bernard watched on separate screens.

Aware a camera was on him broadcasting to everyone else, Lester managed not to flinch when the new window popped up. He saw it was a call from Bernard, looked at Bernard's original window on the conference call, saw Bernard staring intently, eyebrow raised, into his own camera—clearly an expression meant for Lester.

Smiling slightly, Lester answered the new, private call, and a second image of Bernard, this one from a second webcam on the side, appeared. Bernard reached over, picked the webcam up, and pointed it at Johannsen's screen, the latter's head complete with royal crown and pink pig nose.

Everyone's faces on the screens then simultaneously reacted to Lester's as he suddenly let out a loud half-second laugh, which was quickly replaced by a sorrowful, straight face.

"Bernard," Johannsen turned his attention back, now ignoring Chen. "What's your timetable going forward?"

The image of the pigeon coop continued its grasp on the edge of Bernard's mind, a real murder all of twenty yards away from where he had slept, the body hanging upside down, *smiling* over at him—that had kept him from sleeping well for some time now.

He had kept the video game in front of him partially to avoid falling asleep during what promised to be an uncomfortably long meeting, but now he was drafting a work order for Chen Li, one in which a very Johannsen-like avatar would be the target of a jungle hunt.

"Well," Bernard said, taking out and brandishing his iPhone and inserting a definite hint of having been offended into his voice. "It just so happens we are doing a special quality check," he lied, "on the Version 2 plans, and we decided we needed to revamp some things."

Fortunately, Bernard's refusal all his life to admit when he was wrong or had made a mistake had taught him to be a quick, adamant, and, one would have to say, skilled liar.

"Quality check? Revamp?"

"Yes, you see, it was the final quality check that made Version 1 successful," he lied, gesturing with the iPhone, as if that somehow validated his argument. "We considered the overall gaming experience, whether the game contained enough variables, enough subthemes, enough truly enticing graphics . . . and we conducted a final revamping in our plans *before* beginning production. *That*, I'll have you know, is what made our game the huge success that it has been and still is, and it would have cost a tremendous deal more to make those final changes after production had commenced."

"And while you're 'revamping,' as you put it, we are spending *how much* on keeping *how many* engineers in China doing nothing?"

The image of numerous Chinese family members doing nothing on the alley in front of Bernard's house popped into his mind.

And now Bernard did what he always did when challenged. He opened a candy bar, in this case a 3 Musketeers.

Chewing, he said, "I will have you know that engineers in China cost about the same amount of money that you pay your Mexican gardeners to cut your grass in the winter *when it doesn't even grow.*

"As for Mr. Chen," Bernard said, emphasizing a serious expression in his camera, "we could easily cut your team for the interim and hire a new one next month, if you don't have enough to do.

"Now, George," and here he took on a challenging expression for Johannsen, "is it killer games that you want or game killers? If it is killer games that you are after, then understand they come from creativity, from, in fact, play. Should you try to run things like a sweat-shop software business, you will get nothing.

"In fact, your overall tone is no doubt putting my entire staff off, so that it'll be another week before they can work again at full capacity. So I will have to spare us from further distress. Here, I have just sent a new work order to Chen Li that will keep his entire team busy for the next few days.

"Beyond that I would ask you to continue to oversee finances and marketing and distribution and things like that. But in the meantime, leave the creativity to us"—and with a few clicks and keystrokes in the Effects window, Johannsen and Kelly Chambers both erupted in virtual flames (which only Bernard could see), and a further click dropped them entirely from the videoconference.

This was the sort of technology that heads of the world's largest corporations dreamed of.

The engineers and the Beijing team looked on with a mixture of disbelief in the way Bernard had handled Johannsen and of envy in his audacity.

Chen Li opened the email Bernard had just sent, scanned it briefly, and looked up. "Really?" he asked. "And the target character should look like Johannsen?"

"Really," Bernard said. Then, "Hey, Chen Li, I have a question for you: What do you know about raising pigeons?"

"Raising pigeons? My grandfather raised pigeons after retirement. I remember my father said that was his most happy time of life."

"Really? Hmm . . ."

🐦 🐦 🐦

Limei's grandfather, Lao Wang as he was called, sat on the beach house's back porch looking out toward the water as he did each afternoon. He was truly thankful for living in such a beautiful place. Certainly he had come a long way from the village in Sichuan where he lived as a child; and from that tiny flat in the Hong Kong housing project, a studio apartment his entire family was forced to share after fleeing the mainland; and then from an equally cramped apartment in San Francisco after his daughter brought him and his wife over some years back.

And now she had bought the two of them this wonderful beach house, saying their hard work had allowed her to get an education and become successful; now she had the opportunity to pay her parents back.

But he had always dreamed of raising pigeons as his father had, and his father's father had before that. He remembered helping his grandfather train them, his grandfather and father explaining the different kinds of pigeons, and how to feed them and exercise them.

The day Lao Wang built the pen on his roof was one of his happiest, at least for the few fleeting moments before that nasty fat man across the street woke up. That man probably hated Chinese people, Lao Wang figured.

Now he wasn't allowed even to go up on his own roof; the structure was all covered in yellow tape, was an official crime scene, and he himself was a suspect.

No doubt Lao Pangzi (Ol' Fatty) across the street had something to do with the murder. He wasn't tough enough to do something like that himself, but he was mean enough. And who else could it be?

Lao Wang hoped the police would figure it out soon. He didn't want his granddaughter walking around with criminals like Lao Pangzi on the loose.

🐦 🐦 🐦

Ol' Fatty, Grandfather called him. Lao Pangzi. Limei laughed at that.

She laughed at how scared Bernard looked every time he saw Grandmother, too.

But he wasn't such a bad man, it turned out.

He had given her the video game console. And it looked like Grandmother was going to let her keep it, though Limei hadn't said who, actually, had given it to her. She said a boy down the street had lent it to her, which was close to the truth.

Grandparents, while strict, were a lot easier to get to believe something than parents were. Limei probably would have to tell her mother the truth next time she came down from the city.

Limei sat on the little bench next to MoMo's MiniMart and played one of the video games Bernard had given her. She came here nearly every afternoon, telling Grandmother and Grandfather that she was coming to get a soda. Cliff Shores didn't have an abundance of kids her age to hang out with, so she would come here for an hour on her own, to hang out in her own favorite spot.

Except that now Bernard sometimes would come along and have a soda with her and teach her how to play different video games. Once, they were playing a game that hadn't come out yet, and she saw something she didn't like. When she mentioned it, Bernard agreed, and miraculously, two days later he gave her a new version of the game with changes made.

But Bernard hadn't come this particular Monday afternoon, so she played by herself, happy to be out of school for the summer and be in this place, happy to be staying with her grandparents and eating the wonderful food Grandmother cooked every day, happy to have access to all these wonderful video games.

Still, a very dark cloud hung over it all—a man had been murdered and hung on Grandfather's pigeon shed, and that was after the city had ordered the shed down anyway, and Grandfather was very upset about the whole thing.

Life wasn't supposed to be complicated for children, Limei thought.

6

For several days Bernard sat alone in the upper story of his beach house, lost in an orgy of video games, cartoons, movies, and TV shows, usually playing simultaneously on various screens—on the large TVs surrounding the desk, on the laptops, on the desktops, and on several models of tablets.

On one: *Skipping from shadow to shadow, Ninja King (Bernard) effortlessly outflanks his enemies and teammates alike with a skill that younger players did not even know possible . . .*

On another: *"Who lives in a pineapple under the sea? . . ."*

On yet another: *"Caution, speed trap ahead, the police are dropping tire spikes—"*

This game has been automatically paused. You have a phone call from—

Call ignored.

And another: *Pizza Hut, click to order online . . . I'm sorry, we do not deliver in your area.*

The wrappers of frozen foods and candy bars began to pile up among empty bottles of Pepsi, half-empty pizza boxes, and cartons from the few distant restaurants Bernard dared order delivery from.

The Evil Iberian King finds himself retreating from the Balkans, but he has a plan; no, in fact the retreat is a ruse, he flanks to the east, attacks at the enemy's weak point . . .

By the end of the first evening his land-line answering machine had filled up and stopped taking messages, and the voice mail notifications of his various mobile phones were, like their ringers, silenced.

"These are not the droids you are looking for," Obi-Wan says to the lead storm trooper. "These are not the droids we're looking for," the storm trooper repeats obediently.

Even the trips to the minimart had subsided, then ground to a halt, leaving Limei to wonder what had happened to her new friend, and putting a noticeable dent into the shop's revenue numbers.

And every once in a while Lester Argyle or one of the other engineers would find Bernard in a video game world somewhere, be it on a World War II battlefield or the other end of an iPhone air hockey game, but as soon as they revealed their identities, Bernard would switch to another screen, another world, another reality in which to lose himself.

The only person able to keep some track of him was Limei across the street, looking up from her kitchen window at the mass of flickering bluish light shining out the windows above.

🎮 🎮 🎮

"Lahaina Kapana Resort, may I help you?"

"Yes, I need urgently to speak to one of your guests, a Ron O'Brian."

"I'm sorry, sir, but Mr. O'Brian went out early this morning. Both his room keys are here at the desk. Would you like me to ring the room anyway?"

"No! You just connected me to his room a half hour ago! Uh, let me talk to your manager, if I can."

"Yes, sir. Just a minute, sir. I'll put you on hold."

A long two minutes passed to the sound of scratchy Hawaiian music. Then, finally:

"Hai, Jack here. What can I do ya fer?" It was the same voice, but suddenly had an accent.

"Huh?"

"Dees is Jack, da resort manager. What can I do ya fer?"

"I'm . . . uh, my name is Orland P. Kramer. I'm the city manager of Cliff Shores, California. Are you sure you're the manager?"

If Kramer was surprised by the hotel manager's accent, he would have been far more shocked by the appearance. The "resort manager" had dreadlocks hanging down to his elbows, a goatee, and tattoos along both arms—all making for improper additions to the white dress coat and tails he wore.

"What, ya tink I be lying to ya?"

"No, of course not. Listen, we have an emergency here in Cliff Shores. There has been a murder. Our police chief is a guest at your hotel and we need to speak to him immediately."

"Oh, fine. I connect you to his room. Just a mom—"

"No! He isn't *in* his room. Listen, you have to help me. This is official business."

"Ooh, I don't know. It's not *my* official business."

"But I am the city manager of Cliff Shores."

"We have cliffs here, and shores, too—lots of shores. Still, I don't think that makes this *our* official business."

"Listen, we had a murder here. A man was killed and hung on top of a beach house."

"What, you don't have morgues in California? We have lots of beach houses here, but we don't hang no bodies on them."

"No, *we* didn't hang the body on the beach house; the *murderer* did, or at least that's what we're assuming."

"Murder and hanging! My, oh my oh my . . . Cliff Shores must be some evil place. That sort of thing don't happen in Lahaina."

"Yes, well . . . OK, look, uh, Jack, is it?"

"Yep. That be me."

"OK, Jack. We need some special service here—a messenger. And we are willing to pay for it—in fact our emergency dictates we take whatever means necessary to locate and talk with Police Chief Ron O'Brian."

"Pay for it, huh?"

"Yes, and listen, we can view this as a hotel service and be billed by the hotel, or if you'd rather handle it personally—and I like the idea of working *personally* with someone—then we could pay you directly. We'll pay you five hundred dollars for your assistance."

"Five hundred dollars! Woo . . ."

"Yes, if you could help us locate and communicate with O'Brian. Does that sound reasonable, Jack?"

"Sure does."

"So, how soon do you think you can get him on the phone with me?"

"No problem. An hour, maybe two."

"Great. So can I call back at one p.m.?"

"Sure. Just as soon as the money arrives in the mail."

"But we need to talk to him right away. It would take days to *mail* the money."

"No problem. I got lots of patience."

"Jack . . . Do you have a checking account?"

"Yeah, but you have to pay me, not the other way around."

"Listen, if you can provide me with your account number and the routing number, I can have the money wired to your account immediately."

"You can do that? Woo-oo! You must be some real big city manager."

"Yes, and I'll tell you what: This is really urgent, so we'll make it eight hundred dollars. Will that work for you, Jack?"

"Sure thing. You get that into my account and you call back and I'll personally bring the phone to Mr. O'Brian if I have to climb a volcano to find him."

"OK, thank you, Jack. You're a godsend."

"Oooh, nobody ever call me that before."

"Now, give me your account information . . ."

Two minutes later, Jack hung up the phone and walked through the lobby to the lounge. Seated at a table eating brunch and sipping a Bloody Mary was Chief O'Brian.

"Hey, Mr. O'Brian, you gonna get a call in one hour."

"Oh, God, can't they leave me alone? I've got to get out of here. Listen, Jack, you haven't seen me all day, OK?"

"Sure thing, Mr. O'Brian."

"Here, this is for you." The chief handed Jack a fifty-dollar bill.

"Oh, you're too kind to me, sir. I'll make sure I tell them I can't find you, that OK, sir?"

"That's great, Jack." O'Brian finished his Bloody Mary and stalked out of the bar, figuring he had thirty minutes to get his swimming suit on and disappear down the beach.

🐗 🐗 🐗

Kelly Chambers sat at a table in front of the Pig and Whistle pub on Third Avenue in Manhattan. Dripping wet from the humid summer air, she looked indoors with envy, but had opted for a beer at an outside table, where she could secretly sneak bites of a sausage grinder she bought at a stand down the street.

The Pig and Whistle had an extensive menu of classy dishes and likely would frown upon customers bringing in their own grinders.

Leaning down to take a fast, hidden bite of her sandwich and chasing it with a sip of Bass ale on tap, she turned her attention to the folder on the table before her.

The clear-book folder had forty or more plastic envelopes of email printouts and newspaper clippings on the murder. She had been working with George Johannsen to keep an eye on things at the company, and so far, they had been lucky.

The murder had hardly garnered any press beyond one or two local blog write-ups. With a few phone calls, Kelly had learned that all but one of the daily newspapers in the entire San Francisco Bay Area, from San Jose to Oakland, had been bought by a single company in Denver, MediaNews Group.

And wave after wave of consolidation and job cuts had left so little news coverage in the region that a murder could pretty easily go without substantial press beyond local blogs.

Ironically, the Bay Area, the center of the Internet revolution as home to companies ranging from Google to Facebook to Yahoo and more, was among the hardest hit by one of the Web's worst side effects: the death of many daily papers and widespread news coverage.

And better for Kelly, in what write-ups there were, no connection was made to Bernard Walker or OffCide Studios, apparently because no one in the city really understood who Bernard was or how millions of dollars could be invested in video games.

She reread the most-thorough write-up she had found, a posting on the Sunday after the murder, on a blog called the Cliff Shores Scene:

Man Found Dead on Cliff Shores Roof

An unidentified man was found dead Saturday morning on a rooftop on Beach Way, police said.

The cause of death was yet to be determined as of Sunday noon, but the County Sheriff's Department officer in charge of the investigation, Captain Dirk Toland, said the incident was being treated as a homicide.

Toland said the body was found hanging on a rooftop structure, but declined to comment on how the body was removed.

Police are asking the public for any available information on the incident.

In the back of the folder were several sleeves of printouts from tech industry and gaming blogs. The blogs were awash with stories on executives getting into trouble, on stolen iPhone prototypes, and people claiming to own part of Facebook. The bizarre murder twenty yards away from Bernard Walker, CEO of OffCide Studios, would create a circus if any of these publications ever got word of it.

Kelly reflected that they had been lucky so far. Reading, she snuck another bite of her sandwich, only this one without looking up first, and she quickly found her attention turned to a waiter glaring at her, eyebrows lifted.

"Something to eat with your beer, ma'am?" he asked.

7

After more than five days of nearly continuous video games and movies with only short catnaps in between, Bernard finally crashed and slept for a day and a half. He awoke with a sick feeling in his stomach.

For Bernard, being overwhelmed by video games meant really hitting rock bottom.

He had had everything, very briefly. He had put out a wildly successful game, had become rich from its sales, had secured a huge venture funding round and bought the house, had owned a spectacular ocean view . . . for one night—then everything had gone so wrong.

The pigeon coop, the murder, that dead man's face, *the smile,* the mind-boggling behavior of the city, the absence of any credible police response . . .

It had torn Bernard's comfortable world completely apart.

He had even told off Johannsen, the venture capitalist who had personally led the effort to fund his company with a hundred and twenty million dollars and who was now, as a result, a member of its board of directors.

This was what happened to many company founders, his attorney had advised him.

If they weren't very careful, they remained CEO only until they received too much funding from a single party. Then if they didn't act the part, didn't toe the line, they were replaced by some company builder / drill sergeant type who got bonuses the size of Jupiter once they destroyed a company and sold it off, and the founder, the person who had traded away a life's inspiration, the founder was pushed aside and given some obscure title like Chief Genius or Chief Creative Guy.

Well, that damned well wasn't going to happen to OffCide Studios. Bernard had created games that kicked ass compared with the cheap apps people were making billions on on Facebook and smart phones, or the lame PS2 concepts that were still dominating on the high-end game consoles.

After steaming on these thoughts for a time, Bernard jumped out of the lounge chair and sleeping bag.

The coop and murder and city and police had cost him enough trouble, enough time.

Twenty minutes later Bernard stormed into the police station determined not to take no for an answer.

He found Sergeant Peterson at his desk surrounded by a group of angry citizens arguing heatedly.

"My business is down fifty percent since you instituted your stupid parking policy!" one shouted as Bernard walked in.

"Without it the entire downtown gets no business at all, because all the spaces are lost to the beach!" shouted another.

"Right, where *my* business *is*."

"And mine," insisted another.

"Now, now," Peterson said, trying to sound like Andy Griffith but not quite succeeding with his weak, squeaky voice.

Peterson's face grew more dismayed when he saw Bernard appear at the back of the pack. This meeting was not going at all as he had planned—nearly to the point where he was beginning to favor murder investigations over parking squabbles, though the sight of Bernard took the wind out of that prospect, too.

"What's going on with the murder?" Bernard bellowed from the rear, loud enough to silence everyone.

Bernard believed that power lay in making everyone stay quiet while he ranted. He took out his iPhone to give the demand more force.

"*What* have you *learned?*"

All eyes focused on Peterson, wondering what in fact the police had learned about the murder. The fact that a parking squabble was about the most-exciting thing that usually happened in the town—that made an updated report on one of the only murders ever to have happened in Cliff Shores a topic of interest.

What's more, the murder with the aid of the small town grapevine had made it widely known that the new owner of 5 Beach Way was a rich, spoiled video game magnate of some sort. Having the man suddenly appear, shouting murder at the police, united the town merchants from downtown to the beach at least briefly.

Peterson stood up and cleared his throat.

"Pardon me?"

"I said," Bernard repeated, more dramatically, "what have the police learned about the murder? It's been weeks now. Of course, I have only the safety of the Cliff Shores citizenry in mind."

That got nods of appreciation.

Peterson again cleared his throat. "I, uh . . ."

He fumbled for the file, the murder file, one of the only three files in view anywhere in the small office that was, largely, the Cliff Shores Police Department.

"Well," he growled softly, realizing he hadn't cleared his throat well at all. "I have done some investigation . . ." and here he perked up with a determined smile, "and I can tell you I have learned some *pretty interesting things.*"

"And what would that be?" Bernard challenged, undeterred.

"Well," Peterson said, straightening up and rolling his shoulders for effect, which effectively made him look weaker.

"It turns out," he declared like a detective at the end of a murder movie, "It turns out that this is only the *third* murder in the entire history of Cliff Shores."

Bernard's face bloated even beyond its normal bloating, reddened beyond its normal tint. The man had spent all this time learning that?

But to the town merchants, this was in fact enchanting information; it sent them gossiping in a murmur of oohs and aahs.

"Only the *third?*" said one.

"When were the other two?" a woman asked a man next to her.

"I bet I can guess. Now let me see . . ." another jumped in.

"There was Old Man Tyler, the nut who lived up on Dover Hill," said another.

"Oh, that's right. The crazy nut sawed his wife in half."

"No," another broke in, correcting the last in a tone implying a huge injustice, "that can't count. They found Old Man Tyler innocent after the testimony of the character witnesses. They wound up calling it an accident."

"What did the character witnesses say about Old Man Tyler?"

"They didn't testify about *him;* he had confessed. They testified about *his wife*—a perfectly horrible woman."

"So what were the other murders?"

"Didn't one of the town founders escape from jail somewhere back east?"

Bernard looked on in disbelief. Maybe settling in a small town had not been such a wise idea after all.

"Hold it!" he shouted.

The group quieted, looked put out at the interruption.

"Haven't you learned anything about the actual *murder itself?*"

Peterson, who had suddenly gained the confidence of a small town sheriff, now shed it.

"Oh, the *actual* murder. Well, yes, we are looking at a number of questions." He tried to regain his confidence. "For example, who *was* the victim? And of immediate concern, *who* was the murderer? And why *was* the man murdered—and how, by the way? Big, big questions . . ."

And with this he stopped, made a face and nodded his head at Bernard as if to say, see.

"And *the answers* to these questions?" Bernard threw out, as if to say, yes, I see. "Have you learned any of the answers?"

Peterson hadn't thought about that. He became shifty.

"Well, you see, I'm . . . I'm not allowed to comment on certain *details* of the, uh, the investigation," he blurted out off the top of his head, remembering the line from a TV police drama.

"What details?"

"Well, now, good try, Mr. Walker, but of course if I told you what those details were, I'd be commenting on them, now wouldn't I?" he said keenly, like a schoolmarm having just out-debated a student attempting to get out of a test.

"You don't know one thing, do you?"

"Well, now, yes, we do."

"Really? And what would that be?"

"Ah, well, now there's that thing about details we were talking about again. We cannot release details at this point of the *very official* investigation."

"Like who the victim was? Certainly you could release that information."

"It's those county fellows. They don't want to release any detail while the investigation is in progress, you know. It could tip off the bad guys. Sorry."

Bernard searched several of the many pockets on his utility vest, producing two cans of Pepsi and a bottle of Tums before finally coming up with a Hostess Twinkie. He opened it, took a bite, considered throwing it at Sergeant Peterson, thought better of the idea since a small town like Cliff Shores might well have a specific ordinance banning assault on a peace officer with a Twinkie—and put the unfinished portion back into a pocket, after taking another bite.

"Well, sir," he said chewing, "I suppose that in this town, if you want to get something done, you have to do it yourself. I guess *I* will have to solve this murder for you."

Sergeant Peterson smiled. He knew that he himself, a trained police officer, didn't have a clue as to how to investigate a murder; some video game company executive certainly wasn't going to get anywhere.

"I see . . ." he said as if talking to a child, "and you're going to do what we trained professionals cannot? We qualified law-enforcement personnel who have studied criminal justice, forensics . . ." he lied, "and all of that? You're just going to walk in and solve an *actual* murder case? No, I don't think so. Tell me, how much professional experience do you have solving murders?"

All eyes turned to Bernard.

"*Professional* experience?" Bernard said, taking on the sort of look he would get when finding an enemy combatant's weak spot in "Desert War 3."

"Let me ask *you*, Sergeant Peterson, how much money did *you* make solving murders in the past six months?"

All eyes returned to Peterson.

"W-W-Wweelllll . . ." he stammered, "in fact, my salary is a matter of public record. I make . . . well, not a lot . . . but I get great benefits, let me tell you—"

"Ha!" Bernard cut him off. "*I* made more than forty million dollars solving murders in the last six months. And now maybe I'll spend a little of that to solve another."

And with that Bernard swung around and high-stepped his way out of the police department, returning his attention to the Twinkie along the way.

🐓 🐓 🐓

George Johannsen sat in the expensive videoconference center of his Menlo Park office. Facing him on-screen was Kelly Chambers, the chief financial officer of OffCide Studios.

She had a slender face made narrower by her thin shoulder-length hair. In her mid-thirties, she looked young for a C-level executive, but had a seriousness in her face that instilled confidence. Moreover, she was a C-level executive in a company run largely by twenty-year-olds.

"How's the weather in New York, Kelly? It gets cold here in the mornings."

"I'm sorry," she said trying to cover her New York accent. "In California you don't know cold. And you don't know un-comfortable summers. In New York right now it's so humid you have to wring your clothes out before you put them on in the morning."

Johannsen frowned at the image, and at the sight of an open sandwich on Kelly's conference table.

"Eating a late lunch? It's after four, your time, right?"

"Yeah. Just having a quick grinder. It's from this great deli down the street. Now, what can I do for you today, George?"

He frowned more, unsure what a grinder was. George Johannsen was a stereotypical Northern Californian health nut. He looked the very definition of good health and constant good judgment over lifestyle. He had a long head with prominent facial features that readily articulated what he thought about lifestyle decisions such as large, dripping sandwiches between meals.

But fortunately for Kelly, he was all business.

"It's Bernard."

"I was afraid as much. I'm sorry for his behavior the other day. This murder has really affected him emotionally."

"It has affected his judgment, and we cannot have that in a company CEO."

"OK . . ."

"Now I have a substantial investment in the company and I need to be sure it is being safeguarded."

"Yes, sir."

"That's why I need to know I can count on you. I need you to keep a very close watch on everything that is done financially in the company, on everything requisitioned and everything spent."

"Maybe I'd better fly out to San Francisco for a few weeks," Kelly offered, knowing she had to, but hoping Johannsen would say no.

"That would make me feel a lot better," he said, making Kelly feel a lot worse. "I need to be able to tell our other investors we have someone confident watching over things."

"Yes, sir. You can count on me, sir."

"I know I can. I know I can because I know that if we have to make a leadership change in the company, and at this point it is looking increasingly like we might have to . . . well, you may well be the person to take the helm."

"You mean me as CEO."

"I think you have what it takes."

Kelly looked down at the notepad before her and thought a moment. Then, "I'll get an afternoon flight out, or a flight tomorrow morning at the latest."

"Excellent. I knew I could count on you, Kelly."

Kelly didn't know Bernard that well. Her impression was that he was an overgrown teenager who thought only about himself and had terribly strange tastes in clothes, always wearing a multipocketed vest packed with food.

She knew he was some sort of self-professed genius who

apparently could play and design video games better than anyone—
not a talent Kelly saw a lot of use for in life.

And if there was going to be a leadership change, Kelly knew
instinctively she had to be there. She was aggressive, planned to go
to the top in her career. She couldn't pass up an opportunity like
this.

Even a short stint as a chief executive in Silicon Valley could
make a person quite wealthy, and it would at least be a stepping
stone to bigger and better posts.

Still, the thought horrified her. She didn't like flying, and
cost-cutting at the company meant she would have to fly coach—
measures brought on by the recession (and the fact that she was the
only person in the company who had any need to fly).

More important she didn't care much for California, which was
precisely why she was the only person in the company who needed
to fly. She hated leaving New York City and managed to stay based
there on the excuse that the company had three investors on the
East Coast.

Also to the point, she didn't like salads. Every time she went to
Northern California she wound up being force-fed salad after salad,
and some of the things they called salads were far from appetizing.
It was always leaves that rabbits wouldn't touch, topped with tangy
gourmet sauces they called "dressing" and completely void of all
the good things salads should have, should you have to eat a salad,
like cheeses and anchovies, freshly fried bacon and chunks of steak.

Oh, that's right, she remembered. She had twice found cheese
on salads there: *goat* cheese. She hated goat cheese.

California . . . Kelly shuddered.

🎮 🎮 🎮

Francine Lin decided to try again with the video game guy. She
would go straight to his front door and tell him what she thought
of him.

Except that she wasn't altogether sure what she thought of him.
When she had been handed the case, she was told he was some

rich tech guy. She had expected a sports car, a slick suit, an uppity manner, and rudeness.

Instead she had found a very down-to-earth young man, at least judging by the sloppy clothes he wore. He certainly didn't look rich.

But then again he had hardly spoken the one time she had talked directly to him. She remembered she had done most of the talking, that she had been angry and forceful and wouldn't let him get a word in edgewise . . . except that he hadn't actually tried. There was something in the way he looked at her.

And something in his manner, something in his expression, something had slowly deflated the anger right out of her, so that by the time he suddenly and unexpectedly slammed the door in her face, she was losing her train of thought.

Now he appeared not some debonair millionaire but an overgrown kid, and a bit of a slob.

Bernard looked down from his studio when he heard the doorbell. Seeing Francine Lin there, he hurriedly jumped out of his clothes and put on clean ones, realizing as he did that, wrinkled, they didn't look a lot better than what he had been wearing.

As he opened the door all of a minute later, Francine went straight to the point: "I want to talk to you."

"You do?" Bernard asked, delighted to see her again. She was as cute as she had been the first time. Today she wore a businesslike sports coat and he noticed that her glasses were slightly crooked, or maybe it was her nose.

"Yes, I do. And I am *going to.*"

"OK, well, then let's get some lunch."

"Lunch?! I didn't come here to eat. Besides, it looks to me like you're eating already," she said, gesturing at a half-eaten sandwich in one of the pockets of Bernard's vest, which he held in his hand.

"People accuse me of that a lot," he said as he nervously set the sandwich on a moving box."

"Well, I didn't come here to eat. I came here to talk."

"And I have something to talk about, too. Come on," he said.

"I said, I didn't come here to eat lunch."

"Well, if you want to talk to me, you'll get a lot further if *I'm* eating. Come along," he said and began walking.

"Where to?" Francine shouted after him, realizing she would have to follow to talk with him. "I really didn't come here for lunch."

"I know this great little spot. Great food, great ambience."

Seeing little choice, Francine reluctantly followed.

"What I want to talk to you about is that pigeon coop . . ."

She talked pretty much the whole way up the hill to the highway. She told Bernard of the elderly couple's background, of how their daughter had a business in San Francisco and was always traveling, so they helped take care of the granddaughter. She spoke of how raising pigeons was popular in China—and in the United States, as well. And why couldn't he see that and be kind and let his elderly neighbor have this one pleasure?

Bernard didn't comprehend much of what she said, but he listened readily to the wonderful sound of her voice.

"Here," he broke in suddenly, and motioned her to sit on the little bench where he had met Limei. Quickly he went into the minimart and emerged five minutes later with his hands full.

He handed Francine a large cup of Pepsi Wild Cherry, and, re-arranging the items in his hands, a hot dog. She didn't want to take either but saw that if she didn't he'd drop the whole mess.

"I'm really not hungry," she said.

"That's OK. Smell it for a minute and you'll want it. It's a Hellfile Jalapeño Hot Dog. You're going to love it."

She looked at it doubtfully. "What, no mustard?"

"Ah," he replied, "it's better that way with Hellfile Jalapeño Hot Dogs. Trust me."

"I want to talk about the pigeon coop, not about hot dogs. Do you really take girls out to lunch at minimarts?"

"Ah-hah! Now you're talking about going out to lunch with me, not pigeons. That is progress. Anyhow, this turns out to be the best place to eat in town."

"Some town! Let's get back to the pigeon coop."

"OK, good, because that's what I want to talk to you about."

"You do?"

"Yes. The police are never going to solve this murder."

"Sure, they will."

"No, they won't. They don't have the capability. But I *will*."

"You will what?"

"*I* am going to find out *who* murdered that man and get this business over and done with."

"How are you going to do that?"

"Trust me. I shall have little difficulty."

Bernard went on to tell her all about the game "Murder Mystery," which had made him so much money, and how the experience of planning out games like that gave him a unique perspective the police could never manage.

Not to mention technology, and the money and personnel resources to utilize that technology.

Francine thought he was nuts but was quieted somehow by the confidence—bordering on arrogance—he displayed. As his banter picked up, she even broke down and began eating the hot dog, which, she thought guiltily, did in fact taste pretty good.

They sat and talked for close to an hour, the conversation finally veering off topic, to TV shows they both liked, to Harry Potter movies, to Sean Connery, whom Bernard thought was by far the best James Bond there ever could be and whom Francine loved dearly in any role he played.

They then walked back down to Beach Way where Francine's Honda was parked and said good-bye.

Francine felt like she had accomplished something, but she soon realized she had no idea what that was.

🐾 🐾 🐾

That afternoon Bernard again made his way around the back, up the short cement wall, and along the path passing the ritzy Cliffside Condos—to MoMo's MiniMart above.

When Bernard arrived at the minimart, he found Limei on the bench. He sat down next to her.

"Aren't you going to get a snack and a soda?" Limei asked.

"No time," Bernard said as he pulled a ham sandwich out of one vest pocket and a can of Pepsi out of another.

Limei marveled that the Pepsi was clearly iced and wondered how Bernard kept sodas chilled inside the vest.

"I have something to tell you," Bernard said excitedly. "*I* am going to solve the murder."

"What?"

"*I* am going to solve the murder."

"*You're* going to solve it? But how?"

"How?!" Bernard questioned her with an offended tone. "How *not?* I oversaw the design of a multimillion-dollar murder mystery video game. I can certainly do a lot more than these oafs in the Cliff Shores and county police departments."

"But this is a *real* murder, Bernard, not a video game. A man was actually *killed.*"

"Yes, I noticed that. But, listen, putting this real murder into a video game world, we'll be able to look at the pieces and figure it out."

"A video game world?"

"Yes, exactly, with all the modeling, all the characters, the whole neighborhood . . ."

"That sounds like an awful lot of work."

"Not with a software team in China. I'll have it up and running in no time. And besides, the police aren't getting things done any faster."

"Why are you so anxious?"

Bernard started to blurt out how much he wanted to get the pigeon coop removed, thought better of it, and lied instead.

"Well, I want to help your grandfather, Limei. I want to show the police that no one on Beach Way could have had anything to do with the murder."

"You just want to get rid of the pigeon coop."

"Well, there is that, I have to admit."

"A video game world? I don't know . . ."

Bernard stayed with her a few more minutes explaining his plans in between bites of ham and cheese on Wonder Bread, before heading down the hill for his next meeting.

8

"Quickly follow me upstairs," Bernard said to the team assembled at the front door and directly led them up the inside stairwell to his studio above.

A good half a foot taller than the others, Bernard was a commanding figure and had an equally demanding manner.

But any command he held over the four engineers who had driven up from the San Francisco office quickly dissolved when they caught sight of the studio at the top of the stairs.

"Wow, *dude,* what an office!" said Lester Argyle, the company's senior producer in rank—at the age of all of something like twenty-four.

"Yeah, this is awesome, B.," added Tom Dirks as he walked into the wide, open room that spanned entire upper floor. "Whoa, wait, what's *that?*" he asked suddenly, shocked at the sight of the crude pigeon coop across the alley.

A third member of the team, an engineer named Eric Lyle, had had his eyes glued to a PSP console the entire climb up the stairs— cussing lightly as his thumbs worked the buttons in a frenzy.

But the sight of the coop drew even his attention, forcing him to look up.

"Whoa, is *that* where the body was found?" he asked, then returned his attention to the hand-held game console.

"That, *that* is what is causing all of this," Bernard proclaimed. "*That* is where the body was found. *That* is what has wrecked my view. And *that* is what we are going to deal with today."

"Cool."

"Sit down," Bernard said, setting out several two-liter bottles of Pepsi, along with paper cups. To that he added three bags of cheddar-flavored popcorn.

Lester Argyle set a backpack he carried in on Bernard's U-shaped desk, opened it, and produced a small coffeemaker, and without asking picked a spot to set it up, plugged it in, and helped himself to a bottle of mineral water from the studio refrigerator, half of which he poured into the coffeemaker.

Bernard ignored him. "OK, please listen. Here are the facts, what will be the start of our video game," he said, chewing on a Hershey's with almonds. "The body was found there, hanging upside down on that . . . that . . . *thing*," he said pointing.

"A miscellaneously placed pigeon coop?" Lester asked.

"One that appeared just as suddenly as the body did, and did so exactly one week earlier." Bernard added, noting the odd coincidence.

"And his knees were bent back over the top of the thing?" Lester asked. He thought about this a moment, then added, "Cool! Wish I had seen it."

"I wish I had *not*, I will have you know. Now, some more facts. To begin with, one shoe was missing. Next, the coroner said the victim died from a blow to the head but couldn't say if the blow had been inflicted before or after the body somehow mysteriously and silently made its way to the rooftop."

Lester was scribbling notes. "And the neighbor who built the coop lives in that house, right?"

"Yes, along with a perfectly terrifying wife. And a granddaughter who has this cool ancient Game Boy."

"And he built this shack thing to raise pigeons in?"

"That is correct." As Bernard spoke, he opened a bag of cheddar cheese popcorn.

"This would never sell," Lester said, abruptly changing tone. "You gotta start with a concept that is at least *a little* believable, or your video game will never sell."

"Let me continue," Bernard went on, ignoring him. "They have regular visits from family members, though those have suddenly subsided recently. They also say they did not hear a thing. *I* was sound asleep right over there, only about twenty yards from the body, and *I* did not see or hear a thing.

"I woke to see the dead body upside down staring at me—Mmm, good popcorn . . ." Bernard said chewing.

And continued, mouth full: "There is no explanation as to how the body got there or as to whom the victim was, who murdered him, or how." This he followed with a handful of popcorn, and, still chewing, continued:

"These are the starting parameters of our new game. Use the whole team and send anything substantial to Chen Li in Beijing. I need this done ASAP.

"Oh, and one more fact that might be important. The victim was smiling."

"Smiling?" Lester asked.

"Correct. Smiling down at me."

"Cool!"

The discussion went on for a short while longer, with the others asking Bernard questions, except for Eric Lyle, who continued to contest the Cross Country 500 driving a souped-up Ford Pinto on his hand-held game console—but who, Bernard knew, was taking in much of what everyone was saying. This was just the way Eric Lyle was.

When they were through, Lester and Tom took out cameras and began photographing and filming everything, first inside and then out, and then one went to photographing down the alley and the other up the hill toward the main road.

Next they walked the beach taking pictures of everything and everyone they came across.

And as Bernard predicted, Limei's grandparents came out for their regular afternoon stroll, and as soon as they disappeared from sight, he knocked on the front door.

Limei opened it and Bernard hustled Lester inside to photograph their house, including several hundred pictures of the roof and the coop from every possible angle.

And with that the team headed back into the city to begin their work—stopping only for a quick pinball tournament at Bernard's office before departing.

Kelly Chambers sat packed into an airplane seat that made even her thin figure feel cramped. She was staging a psychological battle for dominance over the two arm rests she was forced to share with passengers on either side, figuring since she was stuck in the middle seat, she should get at least that minor comfort.

Kelly was not a happy woman. She had been stuck with a bad seat, had trouble finding a cab, got held up in traffic going to the airport, hit a long line at check-in and another at security, received a pat-down she would not quickly forget (one the patter down probably would not either), had to run to the gate to board her plane—and now found herself sitting on one side next to a man who apparently did not particularly enjoy bathing and on the other a woman whom one glance assured her that here was a person who could fill the full five hours it would take to fly across the continent with incessant talk.

Kelly sighed when the stewardess pushing the drinks cart finally waddled up to her row.

The man who apparently didn't own a shower ordered tomato juice and the talkative woman began explaining in great detail why she had to drink only diet sodas, and it had more to do with digestive problems than it did keeping down her weight, a task that Kelly guessed would have posed an uphill battle anyway.

Kelly managed to call out an order for a double scotch on the rocks.

"That'll be eleven dollars and I'm afraid we take cash only."

"I thought you switched to credit or debit cards only."

"That was a different airline. We take cash only. Cuts down on costs."

"Good thing I used my credit card to *pay for all the baggage fees* and the fee for booking online and all the other fees you people charge. So I have enough cash left . . . to pay for an eleven-dollar cocktail. I could get cheaper drinks at a Yankees game."

The stewardess looked at Kelly condescendingly. "Very well. Here you are . . . And will you be having lunch on today's flight? There's a price list in your seat pocket," she said with a mean tone in her voice.

Kelly recalled being flooded with free drinks and great food while flying business class with her parents when she was a girl, remembered a few weeks earlier reading about the Middle East airline that had sleeping compartments . . .

The drink made her feel a little better, though it got the woman next to her onto the subject of alcoholism and an in-depth account of how her Uncle Harold had been arrested for getting drunk and serenading the mayor's wife wearing only his undershorts—on the balcony of an opera house. And that led to a more-detailed description of the bodily changes brought on by liver disease in her late Aunt Sarah.

In time, lunch was delivered, though Kelly quickly determined the word was probably too strong for what was actually served, and the liver disease conversation had killed her interest in food just as it had her interest in drink.

One part of the plate held what appeared to be bits of chicken in some sort of sauce. Next to that was a small pile of rice and some carrots and asparagus very possibly made of rubber.

Looking down the aisle Kelly could see just the beginnings of the first-class cabin. The seats looked as wide as a California freeway, and a stewardess was cutting slices of roast beef to the particular preferences of the passengers—end cut, pink, more well-done . . .

🐦 🐦 🐦

"That Bernard Walker fellow sure is difficult to deal with," Sergeant Bill Peterson asserted to Captain Dirk Toland. "Now he says *he's* going to solve the murder. Hah!"

"He gets in my way and he'll find himself locked up real fast. You can tell him I said so, Peterson. Besides, he's a person of interest as much as that Wang fellow is."

"Really? So you *have* learned something!"

"There isn't a goddamned clue what happened. It's as if the damned body fell out of the sky—which, by the way, I considered, though a body dropped from even a low-flying airplane would be traveling so fast it would tear the pigeon loft right off the roof."

"So why do you think Wang or Walker might have been involved?"

"Simply because there's no other explanation. And if we don't come up with *something* or *someone,* the public will go nuts. So keep your eye on both of them."

"So what *do* we know?"

"Not a goddamned thing! The victim had no ID. He was dressed in what appeared to be pajamas. We've checked through the FBI and found no match. There are no missing-person reports. The coroner's report finally came in, and they aren't even a hundred percent sure what the cause of death was. Probably hit with a blunt instrument, but when, where—they just can't be certain."

"Oh my . . . So they really found nothing?"

"Well, almost nothing."

"What do you mean?

"They said it was probably a painful death. That's why the face was all tense, like it was smiling."

"Oh my, now I'm going to start having nightmares about that smile again."

"Well, I'm going to go back and do a little harder questioning."

"Oh my . . . Mind if I tag along and watch?"

"Sure. Maybe I'll teach you a trick or two."

🐔 🐔 🐔

The studio looked drastically different than when Captain Toland had seen it last. It did not look in any way more normal, but it was, definitely, drastically different.

Before it had looked like the wake of a hurricane with Star Wars princesses standing about; it now looked like the bridge of a spaceship with princesses standing around.

"Tell me just how it is that you use erotic dolls to make video games," Toland started out in a demanding tone, aiming to put Bernard off guard.

When Bernard had met them at the front door, Toland insisted that they sit down for a prolonged interview—unless Bernard wanted to be taken to the station, where they could wait for several hours for his attorney to show up to be present.

Bernard guessed Toland did not know just how much money he paid his attorney, but he also did not want to spend that much on the attorney, and nor did he have time for the likes of Captain Toland; Bernard Walker had more-important things to do. So he brought the two officers up to the studio, to what was to a degree the crime scene, where Toland wanted to do the questioning.

They took seats around one end of the U-shaped desk, about the only spot other than Bernard's desk chair that wasn't occupied by a screen.

And when they were seated and ready to start, Bernard suddenly got up, walked to the refrigerator and pulled out a piece of fried chicken, which he began chomping on while walking back to the desk.

"How about getting rid of the chicken? And again, tell me about the erotic dolls. Is this some sort of sick hobby?"

Bernard did not like Toland's manner or tone, did not like the insinuation—but he never shied away from a chance to show off his software. Rolling his eyeballs Bernard clicked a couple of icons on a laptop to his right, and three of the large screens came to life.

On a screen to the left, with the help of a little mousework, the famous Star Wars scene of Jabba the Hutt with a captive Princess Leia appeared. A screen to the right lit up with several images of Lego Leias, including one in a white Imperial uniform and one in a Lego-like equivalent of the chain negligee. And on the main screen in front of them several animated models of Leia appeared, each rotating slowly, each showing various degrees of lifelike and animated qualities.

"Now," Bernard explained, "the screen on the left is the real actress in the blockbuster movie. On the right we see an excellent video game portrayal of the character, in terms of animation and modeling. And in the center are various models of the same character ranging from lifelike to cartoonlike."

"You made these?"

"No. I am studying these. These Star Wars games represent the cutting-edge of video game animation, whether simple and cartoonlike or realistic. I study these and compare them with the real statue over here and learn how to add similar qualities to our products."

Toland stared at the screens. He wasn't sure if Bernard was ingenious or just sick. The latter better suited his purpose.

"Is this really how you spend your days? Is this really how you make your living?"

Bernard took another bite of chicken, and, with his mouth full, said, "Is this really how you make yours?"

Then he held up a webcam, first to Toland and then to Peterson, clicking on the laptop to capture images. And with all of about sixty seconds of working the mouse, the images on the center screen were replaced by the heads of the two officers.

"Here, now watch this," Bernard said. He clicked a few more times and in seconds, new images with the two officers' heads began to appear beside the originals, each more cartoonlike, and after three of each showed up Bernard made a final click and a fourth appeared, showing their features on a Lego man.

Toland squinted; Peterson bit his lower lip.

"Simple technology, but it creates new worlds of entertainment."

"Sick," Toland insisted.

"No, no . . ." Bernard countered. "Here, I'll show you sick." And with a few more clicks he added new bodies to the two officers' heads—a Lego Han Solo to Peterson's and to Toland's a Lego Leia body with chain negligee.

Toland turned visibly red; Peterson giggled.

"Anything else you'd like to ask me about the statues?" Bernard asked.

Toland angrily opened up a notebook and crossed his legs.

"So, who is, or who *was,* the victim?"

"*I* have no idea!"

"How did you get him up onto the pigeon loft, and more to the point, why?"

"What do you mean by *loft?* A heap of lumber it may be, but not a *loft.*"

Toland shot back angrily. "So why did you hang the body on the heap of lumber?"

"I did not *hang* the body on the heap of lumber."

"So you didn't mean for it to be there?"

"I had nothing to do with it. I don't know who the man was, how he died, and I certainly don't know how he got up there. As Sergeant Peterson here can tell you fully well, I had every reason *not* to want a body found up there. That monstrosity of a *loft,* as you call it, was due to be torn down the very same morning. That scrap heap has caused me no end of problems, and it frankly has me in a bit of trouble with a prominent venture capitalist."

Toland scribbled in his notebook: *Check for missing venture capitalists,* though he wrote it more because he didn't want Peterson to think Walker had gotten the best of him. That and, well, he wasn't entirely sure what a venture capitalist was.

And after a moment, Toland looked up, glanced at Peterson like *watch this,* and said, "So let's start again. But first, can you turn off those goddamned video screens, for Christ's sake. I'm not into erotica."

"The film was rated PG and the very excellent Lego game over here is rated E for everyone. As for the police officer figures I just made, I am sure they would not fall within the strict, family-friendly guidelines that the Lego company has set for its products."

Toland turned a much darker shade of red.

"Just turn them the hell off. And we're going to sit here all night and go over this again and again until you tell me what I came here to find out, get it? Now tell me again: How did you murder that man?!"

Bernard rolled his eyeballs and turned to the laptop. With some further mousework, all of the Leia images were replaced by live video on the three screens of Bernard himself, taken with the webcam he had shot the two officers with, so that now they were looking at Bernard surrounded by three larger-than-life video images of Bernard.

He held the webcam in front of him, and the real Bernard and the images spoke at once: "I had nothing to do with it. I don't know who the man was, how he died—and I certainly don't know how he got up there. As Sergeant Peterson here can tell you, I had every reason *not* to want a body there. That *monstrosity* that the body was hanging on was due to be torn down the very same morning. That scrap heap has caused me no end of problems, and frankly—"

Toland audibly growled.

"I was recording that," Bernard said, his voice even cockier. "I just thought, since you said you wanted to go over this again and again and again—apparently you are a bit slow—that I could offer you this video. I can put it onto disk for you, you can take it home, and you can study it all night. In the meantime, I'll be able to return to a video game I was playing. I was deeply involved in a match of 'Presidential Paintball,' and I had knocked out the entire Republican slate except for Sarah Palin, who it turns out is especially difficult to beat at that game. She's pretty good with a rifle."

Toland tried to growl louder but instead made sort of a squawking sound, which had a particularly weird effect coming from a guy who looked a lot like a G.I. Joe action figure, all square and mean looking.

He stood and walked to the inside stairwell, gesturing Peterson to follow. Before going down, he turned and glared at Bernard.

"I got your number, mister, and soon I'll have *your butt.* We'll stumble across something, and that's if you don't slip up first. Come on, Peterson. We got what we wanted here."

Peterson followed, trying to storm out in a similar manner, but then stopped by the door, afraid to offend.

He turned and looked at Bernard. "Uh . . . uh . . . cool desk with all those screens, cool software," he said, embarrassed.

Outside, Toland leaned against his car and looked at Peterson.

"That turkey really steams me," he spit out, tension visible in his face.

"I told you. He's a very unpleasant fellow."

"He's a very unpleasant *son of a bitch* is what he is."

"But you have to admit . . . those video screens are pretty cool."

"Those video screens are probably being used for illegal activities. In fact I'll bet that sick kid is running pornographic websites up there. I read up a while back in an FBI bulletin on these Internet porn rings and the sick stuff they put out that children might see just by doing innocent Internet searches," Toland said, the idea of Bernard's possibly being involved in even more crimes helping to ease his tension.

"Oh my . . ."

"I mean, you just google right *into* this stuff. *People's wives* could accidentally find this junk."

"Oh my . . ."

"But we did what I planned. I let him *think* he won the conversation, but I also let him know we are very serious, and that's gonna get under his skin. He's gonna lose sleep tonight."

Upstairs, Bernard finished the chicken breast while deciding whether to do more work on the murder modeling his engineers had created. It was either that or return to potshots with Sarah Palin in "Presidential Paintball."

Kelly resembled the walking dead as she fiddled with the card lock on her hotel room door, finally opening it after several minutes of trying.

She was sick to her stomach when the plane landed. Halfway through the flight she had dared actually to eat some of the alleged chicken and quickly regretted it for the bad taste the "sauce" left in her mouth. And before she could shake the taste off, the plane hit a solid hour and a half of turbulence, shaking up her stomach such that the taste was still in her mouth now, several hours later.

The bad flight was followed by a harrowing trip from the airport. Kelly had rented a car, figuring she had to, as much to get around the maddeningly spread-out Bay Area as to fit in with Bay Area people, whose lives seemed centered around highways.

She quickly found herself completely out of place on the wide freeways, with people whizzing by her on either side. Worse, the five-plus-lane freeways intimidated her with their confusing diamond lanes, cutoffs, and junctions, and Kelly soon found herself completely lost, heading somehow for San Jose, then wound up on something called the San Mateo Bridge—which turned out to be seven miles long—and when she had crossed that and managed to cross back, finally got off onto a side street so she could call her hotel for directions. She noticed many Californians seemed to have no trouble with the idea of talking on their cell phones while driving, but Kelly thought better of it.

She wished her BlackBerry had the GPS systems that came on newer smart phones.

Then when Kelly was checking in, the desk clerk was rude when she said she hadn't in fact actually memorized her license plate number ("It's a rental!"); she was told that, no, hotels do not necessarily have to have on-site dining and that there was a Denny's only two exits back to the north—*on the freeway*—and she was left to walk out to a gas station in search of dinner, or at least something that would erase the taste of airplane "food" from her mouth . . . and now she was entering her hotel room armed with a Salisbury steak microwaveable TV dinner, only to discover that her room did not have a microwave oven.

She opted instead for a scotch on the rocks.

Murders sure were a pain in the neck, she reflected.

9

On Thursday, when her grandparents went off on their daily walk, Bernard snuck Limei up to his studio. She looked around in wonder as she walked in.

For a kid her age, the studio was magical—the large flat screens on wheels, each alight with games or video, numerous laptops and desktops and hand-held devices on the U-shaped desk, the pinball machine, life-size posters of characters from science fiction, cartoons, and video games . . .

Then the view caught her eye, causing first further wonder and second a smile.

"I can see why you don't like Grandfather's pigeon coop," Limei said, chuckling. "But you have to help us. Grandfather would never hurt anyone."

"I can already prove that in this case he could *not* have," Bernard declared. "Look," he said indicating the main monitor on his desk.

To her complete delight, Limei found herself looking at a Limei avatar, one with surprising detail—hair just like hers, a bag like the one she carried, and even a cellphone just like hers—and it was standing in the living room of her grandparents' home across the street, with detail right down to the pictures hanging on the walls.

Her expression faded from ghostly surprise to complete enchantment.

Bernard smiled.

"Use the arrow keys," he urged her.

"No! It can't be!" she said, smiling widely.

"Yes, it certainly *can* be." Bernard opened two bottles of Pepsi and handed her one.

Carefully Limei pressed the forward arrow key and, sure enough, her character began moving forward. She navigated it through the room, halfway up the stairs, back down again, and then over to the door.

"O for *open*," Bernard said when she got there, and Limei pressed the O key, causing the door on the screen to open and let her out. Limei steered her avatar down the alley, then smiled up at Bernard.

"Toggle V for different views," Bernard said.

Limei hit V and found herself seeing the Avatar's point of view looking out at the open alleyway. She hit it again and got a map of the area, showing her location as a little blue arrow. And hitting it again, she viewed her character from above.

"It's wonderful!" Limei said. "But I don't think more video games are going to solve the murder, Bernard."

"No? Have you no faith? Well, press F3, Miss Doubter."

Limei did, and the body of the victim appeared on the ground in front of her.

"Ooh!"

"Fear not, now, this is a video game," Bernard said sternly. "Press P for *pick up*."

She did so. Her on-screen character picked the body up over its head. Limei used the arrow keys to try and walk, but instantly her character melted to the ground, the computer booing her with a "Da-da-da!" in the process.

"The body is too heavy for you to carry, even if you could pick it up," Bernard informed her while chewing on peanuts. "The computer takes into account your sex, height, weight, and age to see how long you would be able to handle the weight of the body."

Limei frowned.

"Don't feel bad. I only held it up a few seconds. That's the thing: No one who lives on this alley would have been able to lift the body long enough to carry or raise it up to the coop."

"Wow!"

"This virtual Cliff Shores hasn't solved the murder yet, but it has proved one thing: Your grandparents are innocent. I am innocent, and *you* certainly didn't put the body up there."

"Oh, thank you so much. But they may still think my grandfather was somehow involved. And . . . and you don't look happy."

"I was just thinking . . . Eliminating all the obvious possibilities doesn't really solve the crime. In fact, it's taking away the only things we had to work with."

🎮 🎮 🎮

Three figures drift smoothly down Beach Way like ghosts floating. When they reach the dead body, the three together pick it up and manage to keep it aloft. They walk toward Limei's house cursing at one another either for not moving quickly enough or for moving too fast.

A large bird floats overhead and one of the three figures pulls out a revolver and shoots it, leaving it to fall right on the body and knocking the deceased and the pallbearers to the ground.

"Damn it, Lyle, what is a weapon *doing in this game?*"

"Heh-heh . . . We added weapons to this segment, Les. Can't have a cool *video game without weapons. Check out what this three-fifty-seven magnum will do to—*"

"Can it! We can screw around later. Right now, we're supposed to be focusing on the murder."

"Aaalll riiiight . . ."

The three figures again hoist the body and struggle to move together inside and in the direction of the stairwell, and they make it about halfway up before one trails behind just an instant too long and the body falls, rolling down the stairs and spurting blood all about in the process.

🎮 🎮 🎮

Bernard, meanwhile, decided he wanted to see how some things worked in the brick-and-mortar world before trusting what his engineers came up with in the virtual one. To this end, he had gone out and bought a rope and a grappling hook and toyed with it, seeing if he could hook it on the pigeon coop from the top of his stairwell.

He learned to whirl it in the air, whipping it about in circles, and finally got up the nerve to hurl it across the way—hooking tightly the top of the coop on his first try.

Maybe it *was* possible for him to have put the body there.

He tugged at it to see if it was secure—then saw the board it was hooked on come loose on one side.

Looking down he saw a woman about to pass by and realized he was about the pull the whole thing down on someone's head.

Bernard waited until the woman was out of sight. He was thinking: Maybe I could just pull the whole thing down—by accident, of course—and get this all done with.

He tugged once more and the board gave way on the side where it had come loose, leaving the grappling hook to fall down and smash into Bernard's kitchen window, cracking it loudly.

"Whoops," Bernard said, and wound up the rope to hang it on the rail. He went inside vowing to keep it—just in case he *should* decide to take the structure down on his own.

Time stretched on, with little further word from the police, but Bernard kept busy working on the case himself.

Each morning he would download a new day's work from Beijing, augmenting the Cliff Shores virtual world. They were getting closer to completing all the streets and buildings between the beach and the highway, and even getting some of the terrain east of the highway where the hills climbed into cliffs.

And each day Bernard would study it, try to be the murderer himself, try to murder the man using different characters, from Limei's grandfather to the girl at the minimart.

He tried to think of new ways the body could have been hung where it was found, new ways it might have been transported . . .

And each afternoon he would carry a laptop up to the minimart and sit on the bench with Limei; eat Hellfire Jalapeño Hot Dogs, frozen microwavable burritos, and cheese puffs; and use the game to brainstorm on how the murder might have been committed.

By the following Thursday he and Limei both had become frustrated.

"We have to think of something new, Bernard," she said finally, over Jelly Bellys and cherry Pepsis. "That tall policeman has been coming around almost every day to question Grandfather. He got that woman Francine to come over and translate."

"Hmm . . ." Bernard mumbled, his attention caught at the mention of Francine. He took a draw off his Pepsi and pictured Francine's messy but cute hair in his mind.

"I don't know if making a video game out of all this is helping," Limei said.

The comment jolted Bernard's pride, brought his attention back to topic. "It helps a great deal," he said, sounding offended. "I would have you know, it puts the murder into a virtual laboratory that allows us to examine circumstances in ways never before possible."

"But you said it yourself: The more we use it, the less we even have to work on."

"You cannot win if you just give up," Bernard responded, picturing in his mind a General Patton avatar leading a swarm of tanks over a hill in the video game epic "Battle Tanks II: The Conquest of Sicily."

"I did not become the world champion of 'TerrorStrike: Crushing the Evil Dictator' by hanging up my game controller every time I ran out of ammo. Now, let's begin again."

"Sometimes I think you're crazy, Bernard. OK. Let's try the murder by going through your house."

"No, we know the body didn't get to the roof that way. I was sleeping in the studio, right where the murderer would have had to take the body out."

They both looked at the laptop monitor.

"The murdered man couldn't have climbed up by himself, right?" she tried.

"Dead men tell no tales, and they equally do not climb buildings, or haven't you heard?"

"No, I mean maybe he was still alive and he climbed up."

"Nope. The coroner's report said he was not in good enough physical condition to climb a small fence. And even if he could have climbed a rope, the only boards it or a hook could have been thrown to wouldn't have held his weight. I'm afraid your grandfather didn't use very good nails."

Limei bit her lips. "So he couldn't have been pulled up, like on a pulley thingy or something?"

"Right, same problem."

"But the top boards held his weight."

"Yes, but his weight was distributed with his legs across three or four boards and the plastic that was supposed to be a roof."

"Maybe he fell from an airplane?" Limei ventured.

"Nope, the coop would have been torn right off the roof, body and all." Bernard stopped briefly, looked down the hill from their bench toward his house below. "Hey, there's a good question: If it came from the air somehow, from which direction did it come? If we can explore that in modeling, then we might get whole new ideas on how it got up there."

"Obviously it had to have come from the east," Limei said.

"*If* it *did* come from the air."

"He could have parachuted."

"No parachute was found."

"Not right on the roof. Maybe it slipped off. Maybe he fell from a very low-flying airplane. Maybe . . ." Limei was sounding desperate.

"OK, look. I'll get our team in Beijing to do some modeling for low-flying airplanes . . . and whatever else they can come up with."

"I'm scared. Grandfather is scared and so is Grandmother. I can see it in their eyes."

Bernard was worried, too. Video games had always solved everything in his life. This latest was not yet doing the trick. He would double his next order from Beijing.

🎮 🎮 🎮

That evening George Johannsen sat across the table from Kelly Chambers at a small, dimly lit restaurant in Menlo Park, the venture capital center just south of San Francisco.

"I want to thank you again for spending time out here, Kelly," Johannsen said.

"I'm glad to be of help," she said trying her best to cover her New York accent.

Kelly looked at the menu with the expression of a tourist trying to make sense of dishes listed in a foreign language.

"What an interesting menu!" she said, consciously trying also to hide a tone bordering between sarcasm and simple disbelief.

Johannsen smiled proudly. "This restaurant is famous for California gourmet specialties."

"Mmmm . . ." Kelly forced herself to mutter. After only a short time in California Kelly was growing hungry. And the thought of California food billed as *gourmet* scared the bejeebers out of her. In her experience so far that had meant well-intentioned but poorly executed mixes of health food, art and, far too often, goat cheese.

Kelly studied the entrées, each of which offered a slightly more-horrifying explanation than the last.

Deep-fried linguine with calamari and organic whole garlic cloves. Pizza with white sauce, fresh shredded ginger, and raisins. Oh God!

"It all looks so wonderful," she lied quietly.

"I am going to have the sweet and sour chicken salad," Johannsen said, showing pride with a head gesture. "My doctor wants to see my cholesterol numbers improve."

God! Kelly hated California. California was the only place where you go out to a restaurant with thirty-dollar entrées and discuss cholesterol.

She had spent the past few days with the small administrative staff at OffCide Studios, and, being polite and businesslike, and ordering what everyone else was having, had endured more salads than she normally would have accepted in a year.

And they didn't even use real lettuce. These salads had leafy weedlike things. Rabbits would go hungry on this fare, she reckoned.

The previous evening, starving, she had stopped at a pizza restaurant next to her hotel. It was called California Pizza Barn and she was soon of the firm belief that the name was a warning, not an advertisement.

"You know, you're right," she said, realizing a salad would save her from having to try and stomach something more substantial, like the avocado-stuffed pot stickers with spicy orange sauce.

"I'll have the same," she said, cringing inside at the thought of sweet and sour sauce on lettuce, or, rather, weeds and leaves.

The gas station next to her hotel sold an industrial sort of hamburger, she recalled, and eased her mind with a promise to buy three on her way home that evening.

"So, what have you learned about company operations?" Johannsen asked while sipping his Italian mineral water.

Kelly sipped at her own mineral water, noticing the glasses of wine in front of nearly every other patron in the restaurant. California made excellent wines; that was one thing she liked about the place. But Johannsen was a health nut and would frown upon the very suggestion that she have a glass.

"Well, it seems that Bernard has been sending projects to Chen Li's group in China—and it's, uh, a lot of them. In fact, the China team has taken on extra engineers."

"What?! *Secret* projects? What projects is he working on if he isn't working on *our next* product?"

"Yeah, well, I'm afraid there isn't a scrap of detail on that in the offices. Bernard is communicating directly with Chen from his Cliff Shores office. All we get in the office *here* is invoices, and the only detail on them is in Chinese. If we want to learn more, I'm guessing I'll have to go to Bernard's Cliff Shores office."

"*Game parlor,* you mean. That's no *office*, from what I hear. What about our local engineers? Can't they tell you what's going on? The China group isn't supposed to be working on anything we didn't design and assign here."

"Yeah, there's that too. Most of our *local* engineers are harder to reach than our China team. Several have been working *remotely*—that's something we don't do a lot of back east. I've talked to one or two on the phone, but there's apparently some *gaming* convention going on in San Francisco."

"Yes, SF Game Expo," Johannsen confirmed.

"And that seems to have largely depleted the office—even the administrative staff."

"Hmm . . . So what're your thoughts on all of this?"

"I'm going to drive out to Cliff Shores myself tomorrow and find out from Bernard directly what he's up to. It could well be legitimate. Maybe he really is doing something on the new game, as he said, and is trying to keep it under wraps."

"Yeah, or maybe this whole mess was caused by that murder that has, frankly, put him out of his mind. I can sympathize with the shocking discovery of the body, but we can't have him running the company if he can't get his act together. And he cannot spend company money on this murder. Frankly, that would mean we need not a CFO like you managing things but a legal counsel.

"If he is spending company money on the murder," Johannsen went on, "Ol' Bernard'll quickly find his title changed from chief executive officer to chief *janitorial* officer."

Kelly took a long drink directly from the four-dollar bottle of mineral water Johannsen had ordered for her and sighed in a very strong New York accent and with a very strong note of sarcasm in her mind-set.

And then she blanked her mind with the professionalism she had come to perfect in her career, and looked Johannsen in the eye.

"Either way, I'll find out, and meet with you again tomorrow evening."

"Great. I knew I could count on you." Johannsen wiped his mouth with his cloth napkin, set it on his lap, and straightened his posture.

"Hey, we could have dinner together again tomorrow then!" he blurted out.

"Oh . . . uh, *great.*" Kelly said, feeling nauseated.

🐾 🐾 🐾

Bernard had gotten Francine Lin's phone number from Limei on the pretense of wanting to ask if she had learned anything from the police.

He planned to use the same pretense in persuading Francine to have dinner with him. It wasn't that he was underhanded; he was just shy when it came to girls—perhaps the only thing that Bernard Walker had ever been shy about.

"I was just about to go out," Francine said right after answering the phone.

"I'll be fast then. I want to meet with you to discuss the murder case. We could have lunch tomorrow maybe. Or dinner. I mean, as long as we're out."

"Listen, Bernard, I've been thinking. I almost enjoyed having lunch with you that day, but I can't see you as long as you're going to insist on having the pigeon coop torn down. I'm sorry, but you're destroying an elderly man's dreams." With that she hung up.

"Damn . . ." Bernard said under his breath, looking gloomily out at the rooftop structure that seemed determined to ruin every aspect of his life, even this.

10

The three figures argue all the way up the inside stairwell but manage to keep the body aloft as they enter Bernard's studio.

In reality, two of the figures are in their respective Daly City townhouses, just south of San Francisco, and the third is on a beach near the Golden Gate Bridge, but in their minds, in their hearts, and on their laptops they are carrying an oversize dead body into the private studio of their boss.

"Ssshhh!" Lester Argyle says, nearly dropping his end of the body as he gestures for silence.

They all eye the virtual Bernard, who is sleeping soundly on the lounge chair next to the door. He is snoring quietly, the rise and fall of his chest threatening to knock a half-eaten meatball sandwich to the floor.

The group moves slowly across the room and gingerly tiptoes around Bernard and to the door.

"Hold it here," Les whispers, and with one hand slides the door open. "OK, let's move out."

As they move out to the landing at the top of the outside stairwell, Les eyes the target, the coop across the alley.

"OK," he whispers loudly, "on three we hoist the body toward the coop."

"Ready? One . . . two—"

"Hey, hang on a second," Eric Lyle says, and, reaching back with his Avatar, attempts to move the meatball sandwich on Bernard's chest into a safer position—forcing Les to overcompensate and lose control of the body, which then rolls violently down the outside stairwell spurting blood everywhere, making enough noise to wake the Bernard avatar up—which in turn sends the meatball sandwich to the floor—and setting off a loud, "you lose" duh-duh-duh to echo across the sky.

"Damned," Les says, "Now we have to go back down and start over."

After two bowls of Frosted Flakes and one of Captain Crunch (his doctor had told him to vary his diet), Bernard sat anxiously before his computer. An updated version of modeling was downloading from Beijing.

He had asked specifically to add in every conceivable way of climbing onto the rooftop structure, along with some aerial approaches, all using realistic parameters: size, weight, velocity, strength of various parts of the pigeon coop, number and length of nails used—everything they could think of.

Sipping from a coffee mug filled with Pepsi, he checked the progress, then glanced again at his email.

The doorbell rang.

Bernard took offense at the prospect of someone ringing his doorbell at this hour of the morning. It was only one o'clock in the afternoon, for Christ's sake.

He stomped to the door, swung it open abruptly.

"Hello, Bernard."

It was Kelly Chambers. Chambers was supposed to be safely off in New York, far, far away. That was why he had insisted on hiring Kelly. Aside from her impeccable education and success-ridden career, the more-essential qualification in Bernard's eyes had been her stated refusal to move to California, where, no doubt, as chief financial officer she would be constantly in his hair.

So what was she doing at his front door at an unthinkable hour of the morning?

"And what, may I ask, are you doing here?" he asked rudely.

"I'm sorry, Bernard, but I have to get briefed on certain company details," she leveled at him, tough and to the point, but somewhat wearily. She had not eaten or slept well in days and had not had a pleasant drive to Cliff Shores, a route that followed a narrow-lane freeway that wound up and down through thick woods, then a one-lane highway that wove through Christmas tree farms and, for some reason, numerous antique shops.

"You flew out from New York to do that? We spend several hundred thousand dollars on videoconferencing systems so that you could fly out to get briefed on something?"

Kelly sighed. "Thanks for the welcome," she said sarcastically. "If it makes you feel any better, I had a particularly dismal flight out, and I got lost twice trying to find Cliff Shores. When I lie down to go to bed tonight, the voice of the GPS navigation system I bought for the drive is going to be ringing in my mind: 'Make a legal U-turn, make a legal U-turn . . .'"

"OK, then I do feel better. Now, what is it that you need?"

She shook her head. "Look, can we sit down? And is there *any* chance we could maybe find something to eat in the process? My hotel's complimentary breakfast this morning wasn't very complimentary. Granola, bran muffins, and brown bananas. And it's one o'clock already. I *need* lunch."

Weak from hunger, she only now realized Bernard was wearing a bathrobe.

"You're just getting up?"

Bernard took on an offended look. "This is my work attire. I am trying my best to honor the office spirit despite the fact that I have been working at home as of late."

"Honor the office spirit?" Kelly asked, not understanding.

"Yes. Casual Fridays. And it's not easy to dress *down* from *my* normal attire."

God, Kelly needed food. She wasn't going to handle Bernard if she didn't get some.

"Got anything to snack on?" she asked desperately.

"Snack?" Bernard asked. "If we have to discuss work, we might as well have a *proper* lunch."

"A *proper* lunch?" Kelly ventured, worrying over what West Coast gourmet dishes Bernard Walker was likely to present.

Fifteen minutes later they were seated on the minimart bench, both largely failing to control the toppings they had piled onto their foot-long Hellfire Jalapeño Hot Dogs. The table held two more dogs, equally loaded, along with chips, fresh baked pretzels, and two large cups of Pepsi.

"You were right—mustard would have ruined it," Kelly said, gulping down bites and nearly smiling for the first time in a while. "Thank God. I haven't had a decent meal in days."

"Actually, I contacted the franchise owner and complimented him on, particularly, the excellent selection of potato chips," Bernard said. "In the process I learned that the Hellfire Jalapeño Hot Dogs are bought from a small company outside of San Diego that imports special types of hot peppers from Mexico."

"Wow."

"While talking to the owner, I did, unfortunately, find it necessary to complain about the sorry state of the condiments bar on two different occasions in recent weeks . . ."

Kelly raised an eyebrow, took another bite of her Hellfire Jalapeño Hot Dog hold the mustard.

Bernard went on: "You've no doubt heard about the murder. It has caused me no end of trouble. The murder and the pigeon coop that preceded it."

"I've heard," Kelly said, sort of, her chewing drowning out the words.

"This store is the one good thing that has happened to me in this murder. Do you know that they have *seventeen* varieties of drumstick-style ice cream cones? I counted them. *Seventeen!* And they have these Popsicles that I'd never seen before."

The two continued eating with Bernard expounding upon the virtues of the minimart and Kelly getting the serious feeling that this was not a corrupt businessman embezzling money from a well-funded startup. Bernard simply wasn't mature enough.

And Bernard got the feeling he had wiped away whatever momentum Kelly might have gained by turning up unannounced.

Then, "They don't have fresh chocolate-coated bananas, do they?" Kelly asked. "A fresh chocolate-covered banana would go real well right now."

Bernard choked slightly on his hot dog.

"No." He thought for a moment. So much for turning momentum. Was this a challenge? "You know, I shall be sure to make that suggestion with the franchise's owner the next time I contact him."

Kelly smiled. "I thought not."

"I suppose you have corner markets *this* large in New York City?"

"None that I have to climb through hedges and jump a wall to get to, no. Oh, and this is a highway. You guys don't *have* corners. Or, apparently, geometry teachers."

"You're talking to a video game designer about geometry?"

"I'm talking to a video game designer about managing a company."

"Ah-hah," Bernard said, looked at her intensely, about to reply, then took another bite of his hot dog instead.

Kelly smiled. And instead of beginning to drill him about the company, she steered the conversation in a different direction.

"I go to this deli that has Italian sausage, spiced with fresh hot peppers—whole chunks—and what they do is, just before lunch, they cook batches of fried onions and green peppers and add them onto sandwiches fresh off the grill. Then they top the whole thing with mozzarella—fresh mozzarella, not packaged supermarket stuff—and roast it for a few minutes to melt the cheese."

Bernard squinted.

"But I never thought to hold off on the mustard. Holding the mustard lets through the jalapeño flavor."

She lifted her Pepsi and drew at the straw.

Bernard widened one eye and took another bite.

Halfway into the second round of hot dogs, Bernard finally forced the issue.

"So you have come for what, other than to thank God for Hellfire Jalapeño Hot Dogs?"

"Bernard, I'm sorry—and first let me thank you from the bottom of my heart for this meal—but we may have some problems."

"Problems?" Bernard asked.

"Yes. The way you're running the day-to-day right now. No transparency and every sign of excess. I've begun to think maybe you spent all that money on videoconferencing equipment so I wouldn't be here where I could watch what's going on first-hand."

"And you *have to* watch everything?"

"I *am* the chief financial officer, Bernard! Yes, I do. And like you, I have to answer to our investors. But *unlike* you, I do not have a nifty oceanside office where I can escape to to avoid the world."

As she said this, Kelly looked longingly at the view, a huge improvement over that of the hot dog truck she normally ate at back home, which usually was parked between a large water pumping facility and a thrift shop.

"Studio," Bernard corrected her.

"What?"

"Oceanside *studio*, not *office*."

"Oh. Yeah, whatever."

"And there are in fact things you *can't* know all of, at least not right away. We have to keep the utmost secrecy in video game development. We have bloggers, reporters, and all sorts of people trying to fetch details before we're ready to have them known."

"You don't hide things from your chief financial officer."

"We are not *hiding* anything."

"Oh yeah? Then why is it that on most days I can't locate a single OffCide Studios engineer. Their voice mail keeps telling me they're in workshops at some gaming conference, or at a presentation lunch or a seminar. Well, damn it, I'll go to wherever they are and talk to them between appointments if necessary."

"Then why don't you?" Bernard challenged her.

"I can't," she shot back, "because no one will tell me *where* I can find them."

"What?" Bernard asked incredulously. "They don't *have* to tell you. They already have."

"What are you talking about?"

Bernard set his hot dog down and took out an iPhone. In seconds he produced a map of San Francisco's financial district, one littered with red tags.

"Here, see the letter A?" He touched it with his finger and a box popped up. It read: "Lester Argyle, OffCide Studios, Producer, @ Bayview Lobster House, business luncheon."

"And here . . ." Bernard pushed the B tag several blocks up the street on the map. Another box opened, reading: "Eric Lyle,

OffCide Studios, Design Engineer, @ Maymont Hotel Conference Center, seminar."

Bernard shot Kelly a triumphant look.

"I don't know how you do business in New York, but here in the Bay Area we don't *have* to ask where people are."

Kelly sincerely hated the Bay Area. She sincerely hated iPhones.

"Don't your employees object to the invasion of privacy, your following them around like that?" she asked.

"What *object?* They check in on their own. They *want* to be seen in these places, in these meetings. It helps their careers and lets their friends find them."

"OK . . . Anyhow, I am here with you now. And specifically what I want to find out is what are all the projects you have the China group working on now?"

"Ah, yes, well, that's a secret," Bernard said.

"Can you confirm they're related to 'Murder Mystery 2' or some incarnation of 'Murder Mystery 1'?"

"Ah, well, there's that thing about this being a secret again," Bernard responded with a smile, stealing a line from Cliff Shores police spokesperson Bill Peterson.

Kelly continued. "I had George ask me specifically to find out what you have going on."

"And that is need-to-know only. We're in the final stages of development on a new game, and that means lockdown. Lockdown is what tech startups do at crucial moments, it's what smart companies do when negotiating mergers, it's what companies . . ." Bernard started to say "what companies do when they have top management issues," but thought better of it. Instead: "You are not a designer, so you don't *need* to know."

"Wrong. (A), I control the purse strings in this company, and (B), George Johannsen controls everything in this company. *We both* need to know."

"(C), Johannsen does *not* control everything. I am chairman and chief executive officer—in addition to being the founder. And *I* control *you.*"

"You may find yourself fighting for those titles. It happens in a lot of startups."

"Are you threatening me?"

Kelly looked Bernard in the eye, ready for a fight, but instead took another bite of her Hellfire Jalapeño Hot Dog.

"Definitely don't want to add mustard," she muttered, shaking her head and shaking off the fight at the same time.

She decided against pressing. She had a solid backup plan. She'd simply wait until evening, when Bernard would be going to bed or busy playing video games, and she'd call Beijing herself. Chen Li would tell her exactly what they were working on over there, or she'd put all payments on hold. Bernard wouldn't learn about it until tomorrow, if he even did learn about it, as detached as he was from the company.

The hot dogs, she noted, had made the horrible drive to Cliff Shores worth the trouble.

"As long as I'm down here," she said in a wholly softer tone, "how about a quick tour of this crazy studio of yours? Everyone talks about it."

🐔 🐔 🐔

Bernard wasn't the only person keeping details to himself, though he was doing so far more successfully than Captain Toland.

"Cliff Shores Police Department, Peterson here."

"Hey, Bill, it's Dirk Toland. We'll be coming down again tomorrow for another round of questioning with this Mr. Wang."

Toland liked to have Peterson around, partially to have a greater show of manpower and partially because Peterson seemed to worship him and he got the chance to show off.

"I thought you said you didn't have any clues. Have you learned something new?"

"Well, let's just say that Wang is a prime, and I say *prime*, suspect."

"Really!"

"Unfortunately, I can't give you any details."

"Oh, that's too bad."

"But let me just tell you, I think we're beginning to get the picture."

"Oh, my . . ."

"Yep. This is one of the weirdest crimes I've had the pleasure—uh, the honor to—um, investigate. But the pieces are finally beginning to fall into place, things are finally beginning to add up."

"Absolutely fascinating."

"Myself and our team here at County, we've met pretty extensively over the last couple of days, gone over everything with a fine-tooth comb, and I think there's going to be some movement soon." He neglected to add that the "team" consisted of him and his own supervisor, who chewed him out for moving so slowly.

"Can you tell me what sort?"

"As I said, we can't disclose details at this point in the investigation, even to a fellow officer not directly involved in our meetings. Sorry, Bill."

"Hey, I understand."

"Let's just say that Wang had better get himself a lawyer."

"Ah, so you may arrest him soon?"

"Now I didn't say that, Bill. But let's just say he had better pay attention to those late-night bail-bond commercials."

"Late-night bail-bond commercials?" Sergeant Peterson was usually in bed by nine-thirty. The notion of late-night bail-bond commercials intrigued him.

"Yep. And we think we have a fair picture we can paint in court. But I really can't talk about it . . ."

Toland went on to further insist all details were confidential and in the process pretty much divulge every one of them thoroughly.

As it turned out Toland had nothing really to go on, no evidence that could convince a jury that Limei's grandfather had killed the murder victim, no motive, no murder weapon . . . But he could convince the town and even the local community newspaper that they had found the killer—whom that innocent-until-proven-guilty nonsense would let out on the street, possibly to hang more townsfolk from bird lofts.

Oh, he did have one other motivation for making the arrest: His supervisor ordered him to make one soon.

🐦 🐦 🐦

The lobby of the Lahaina Kapana Resort & Inn was quiet—normal for that time of the day.

A few beachgoers had wandered into the lounge for drinks. Another sat in the lobby in front of a TV, paying more attention to his smart phone than the surfing contest being shown.

Jack had just taken over at the front desk, relieving the day clerk. He was the manager of the resort but preferred working evenings, and got to on the excuse that guests had greater needs in the evening versus the morning. But in reality Jack just liked to sleep late.

The phone rang.

"Lahaina Kapana Resort & Inn, Jack de resort manager here. What can I do ya fer?"

"Hi, Jack, it's me again, Orland Kramer, the city manager of Cliff Shores. You promised several times to get our police chief on the phone for me."

"Oh, yeah, Mr. Kramer, sir. Boy, I am sure sorry but Mr. O'Brian gets up and goes out before any of our staff come on. We close our lobby every night at ten. And then I go to his room two nights this week but he's not there. I think maybe he and his wife may be spending time at another resort. But I got the money you sent to my account."

"I see . . . Listen, can you see if O'Brian's in the hotel right now?"

"Sure thing. Let me put ya on hold, OK, sir."

Jack pressed the hold button and looked over at the lounge. Sure enough, O'Brian was perched at the bar with a tall beer.

Jack waited a moment, then got back on the line.

"No, I'm sorry again. His key's at the desk and no one's answering da phone in his room. Ya want me to try his room again tonight?"

"No, that's all right," Kramer said quietly and the line went dead.

"Woo, boy, he be angry," Jack said with a whistle.

He hurried across the lobby and into the lounge to where O'Brian sat hunched over his drink. Despite the gaudy aloha shirt, his appearance still commanded respect. His roundish body hunched over the bar but had a rock-solid quality about it, and his face seemed to say "I'll bite your head off if you bother me."

"So sorry, Mr. O'Brian, that city manager fellow, he called again. He seem super angry."

O'Brian looked up with an irritated expression.

"Can't I get any peace, Jack?" he pleaded.

"I think they want you real bad, sir."

"Well, thanks, Jack," O'Brian said handing him a twenty-dollar bill. "But our room is booked for another week and we lose the time share if we don't use it now."

A figure appeared behind them, the man in the lobby who had been on his cell phone:

"I think we can get along just fine without you, Ron—permanently."

"What?" Jack said startled. "Whoa, who are you?"

"Orland Kramer," the figure said, eyeing the twenty-dollar bill folded in Jack's hand. "City manager of Cliff Shores."

🎮 🎮 🎮

Kelly Chambers sat in disbelief in Bernard's studio. Bernard showed her the Princess Leia avatars on different screens the same way he had shown Toland and Peterson. But he went on to show her others, also in multiple versions from photolike to cartoonish, including some of himself.

(She also found it comforting that he did in fact have some business use for the life-size statues, especially the one of Leia, dressed in chain lingerie from the Jabba the Hutt collection.)

Kelly had never had any interest in video games, had rarely seen any of the possible graphics. And here she was seeing on several large screens just how the games and graphics were created, along with the software that created them.

And the studio. The comic book character Richie Rich was the inspiration, Bernard told her. Pinball, TVs all over the place, posters, laptops and game consoles everywhere . . . It looked like the home of a bachelor NBA star who was about twelve years old.

And while Bernard had otherwise been arguing with her, again the chance to show off his studio and software brought him to life. He suddenly took on a childlike innocence and—she didn't want to say it—charisma, the moment he turned on his equipment and began explaining.

It wasn't showing off, she noted. It was genuine enthusiasm.

"Can you do one of me?"

"Certainly," Bernard said. "In fact, possibly we should have animated avatars for all management on our website, instead of still photos."

"That would be clever."

Kelly looked to the windows. Her eyes couldn't avoid settling on the pigeon coop, and there was no doubt that it was the spot.

"So that's where . . . you found the body?"

Bernard looked over, angry that the awful structure had interrupted her interest in his work.

"Yes, that is the monstrosity, to whose complete destruction I am committed."

"That must have been an awful shock."

"That would be an understatement. Imagine finding that shack in your view."

"I mean the murder."

"Oh, yes, the body was also quite inconvenient. I haven't slept decently since. And I won't be able to rest until that *thing* is taken down."

"It really does destroy the view."

"And it is totally illegal, not up to code, no permit, nothing. It should be removed immediately, but the police obtained a court order barring anyone from touching it until the stupid crime is solved."

"Hmm . . . I have to bring this up, even if it seems insensitive, but it is a very good thing the press hasn't caught on to this. The founder of a well-funded company turning up with a body . . . hanging like that . . . right next to his . . . studio. Some of the tech blogs would have a field day."

"I have half a mind to call them and inform them of the incident. Maybe with hordes of reporters running around town, the police might be encouraged to get off of their well-settled behinds and do something."

"Don't you dare call them."

"I'm tempted."

"Well, don't. The company doesn't need the distraction— what, with the new game being put together and so forth. Say, when is that going to happen? We have to begin planning for production, marketing, distribution . . . All that takes time and everyone's shut down until you decide to proceed."

"Well, everyone's going to have to wait longer, I am afraid. We are in the midst of making some fundamental changes," Bernard lied, "that will ensure the game's success. And I'm completely unable to focus properly as long as that cursed bird house is still out there."

Later that afternoon as she was driving back over the hills into the city, and struggling not to get lost, Kelly realized the visit had vastly changed her impression of Bernard.

He had always seemed self-centered, rash, arrogant, childish.

But seeing him today in that room he called a studio, she could see why he had received a hundred and twenty million dollars in funding. There was something—and Kelly didn't want to use the word—*genius*-like about him, something that set him definitely apart.

Now she had to go and face Johannsen and rabbit food. She honestly hoped she wouldn't learn anything bad from Beijing when she called that evening.

11

Three large virtual cannons are being maneuvered for position, a little to the left, a little to the right, then up slightly, then back a foot.

One is positioned on Beach Way just down from the Wangs' house, a second is on the opposite side, on the beach, and the third is halfway up the hill toward the minimart.

That final one is the most difficult to aim: move a little up or down the hill and you have to re-aim altogether . . .

There is little concern over the wind, though, given the nature of the ammunition, and soon all three avatars report ready to fire.

"Let 'er rip, Eric," the Lester avatar commands.

A loud bang echoes from the hill, and half a second later an oversize dead body shoots through the air, arms flapping, and splats against the beach house's upstairs window, smashing the glass, then falls to the street below.

"Next!" the Les avatar shouts, and a second body, this one from the beach, soars into the sky. Limbs waving, it climbs, arches, and falls straight down, just narrowly missing the pigeon coop and splatting on the ground in front of Les's cannon.

Now Les fires and a third large dead body bursts into the sky, smashing into and demolishing the coop and continuing its flight out toward the water.

"Damn. Too much powder that time," Les says. Then adds: "What the heck, fire at will!"

And the sky is quickly filled with a steady bombardment of large, arm-flapping dead bodies, splatting on and around the beach house, a barrage that continues with a vengeance long after the final vestiges of the pigeon coop are knocked off the roof . . .

Bernard and Limei spent the afternoon working on the game, trying different routes to transport a large dead body through the neighborhood—unseen—from various points.

And most important they experimented with every plausible method of getting the victim into the air and onto the coop—and left hanging precariously upside down.

In one scenario, the victim avatar, still alive, manages to throw a rope with a grappling hook to catch it on various boards on the pigeon coop. He then would resolutely climb the side of the house, but never make it more than a few feet before falling on his head and bleeding to death on the street, often with the coop plummeting down on top of him.

In another he jumps from a low-flying airplane, comes sailing down like an oversize Superman, and knocks the rooftop structure into a hundred pieces that spread for blocks. And in yet another he parachutes down, which still breaks up the coop, and also pretty much guarantees he would land right-side up anyway.

In another, Bernard operates Phil the Tree Guy in a virtual crane, which even has "Phil's Tree Service" printed on the side. Phil lifts the body on a hook from the crane, gets up above the coop and into just about the correct position, and he is just about to lower the body onto the boards, when Phil suddenly leans over the side and vomits, and instead of the normal losing *duh-duh-duh* echoing through the sky, they hear instead a laughing *duh-duh-duh*—the voices of Lester Argyle, Tom Dirks, and Eric Lyle.

Bernard swore he would get back at them for that.

"It *could be* a parachute. Maybe he got caught in the parachute lines and wound up upside down," Limei ventured.

"No," Bernard replied. "The simulations show otherwise."

Bernard worked on. In another scenario, the victim tries to leap from the top of Bernard's outside stairwell . . . and promptly goes *splat* on the street, spewing blood all over the place. Bernard decided he would definitely compliment Chen Li on the effects.

In another the man throws a rope from the top of the stairwell and ties it to the rail. He then tries to climb across, gets halfway, then splats down onto the pavement, dying, thankfully, before the entire pigeon coop comes plowing down on top of him.

It was Bernard's best theory, so much so that he even continued to play with the real grappling hook, and kept it on the outside rail, just to better contemplate the possibility.

But no. The new additions to the modeling had been very successful in disproving every conceivable theory, and helping Limei and her grandfather in no way whatsoever.

🐦 🐦 🐦

At six p.m. Kelly Chambers was all alone in the headquarter offices of OffCide Studios, though to be fair, the building seemed more like empty office space than a company headquarters, and in terms of decorations and equipment looked much more like a college dormitory than an office.

Kelly had waited till six in the evening to match up with Beijing's morning, remembering that the team there actually came into an office and actually did so during normal business hours—at nine a.m.

Kelly wasn't anxious to rush out of the office, anyway, since her evening would be spent over salads with George Johannsen. The taste of hot dogs lingered on happily in her system.

She sat in the videoconference room, a tablet open before her. She realized she was using the very equipment that Bernard had spent entirely too much money on to keep her at bay, and more ironic, he had personally taught her how to use it.

At a few minutes after six, she got Chen Li on the video-conferencing system.

"Chen Li, how are you?" she asked.

"Good. How are you? What time is it there?"

"It's six in the evening here. Listen, I need to review your recent job orders from us."

"I'm sorry. I don't understand. Can you repeat?"

"I want to ask about our orders to you," she said louder, as if more volume might make her more-easily understood by a nonnative speaker.

Chen Li instantly looked nervous. "I don't know if I . . ."

"It's just to reconcile our books. It's a sort of audit I like to do every year, just to make sure we're recording things right. I'll only need a little information."

"I can send you a list of projects then, though everything we've done has been for the new 'Murder Mystery' game."

So Bernard had not been lying? Kelly wondered. Or did he have the China team lying with him?

"Really? What has the work been? Modeling, polishing?"

"New models. We've been creating the game's great new models, all was Bernard's orders. He said he very anxious to start production the game."

Kelly pictured herself telling George Johannsen that Bernard was in fact doing exactly as he was supposed to be doing, but didn't think Johannsen would believe it.

Then a sudden thought: "Say, can you show me a few of these models, or stills at least?"

"Sure," Chen said, "they're all of the same area." He typed away at a laptop before him and a moment later a demonstration screen sitting next to Kelly lit up—to show not the planned scenes from "Murder Mystery 2," but rather the dilapidated beach house and pigeon coop across from Bernard's.

Bernard shook his head. Nothing made any sense.

The latest modeling of the alley was complete, no details missing.

And it was certain: The weight of the murder victim alone would have pulled the boards right off and sent him flying down the street below had he not been very lightly placed and placed just right.

Conclusion: There was no way the victim could have climbed, or have been carried, to the position he was found in. Not from below and not from Bernard's apartment.

Conclusion: The victim had to have come from above somehow.

Bernard looked out the window at the structure, then down at the house. He felt helpless, unable to help Limei, or her grandfather. And he felt responsible, though he wasn't sure how. But the fact that he had started a fight over the blasted pigeon coop somehow pitted him in the middle of everything.

He pictured Limei's expression when he had broken her old Game Boy, and felt a knot build in his stomach.

🐦 🐦 🐦

Kelly Chambers had briefly jumped at the suggestion that they have something "naughty" for dinner, as George Johannsen said they were going to the best hot dog stand on the Peninsula.

She didn't normally eat hot dogs twice a day, but then again she didn't normally eat salads twice every day, as had largely been her routine here, either.

And now as she found herself looking at a tofu hot dog with melted goat cheese on a slice of whole-wheat sourdough french bread, she wished she were dead.

When people pushed something unidentifiable on her at Chinese restaurants back home, she could get out of it by saying she was a vegetarian.

But what was she going to say now? "I'm sorry, I don't eat tofu for religious reasons"?

She wondered briefly if there was a religion that worshipped bean curd. The religion of the Druids, perhaps.

And at least when she did get forced to eat something un-identifiable at a Chinese restaurant, she was smart enough not to ask what it was. Things tend to taste a lot more like chicken when there is an outside chance that they might in fact have come from something at least partially resembling a chicken.

Kelly struggled to take a bite.

"So," Johannsen said, "what did you learn?"

They had spent the time waiting for their orders by going table to table talking to patrons in the small restaurant, all of whom Johannsen knew and had done business with.

It is amazing how popular a person is if he has a few hundred million dollars in funds that he can invest in other people's companies, Kelly thought. It was also pretty incredible how much business, it appeared, was done in Silicon Valley cafés and restaurants.

Then as they began their dinner: "Did you find out what Bernard is doing with all his time, and all of the company's money?"

Kelly's throat hurt as she sought the words.

She liked the idea of becoming CEO, she liked the idea of running a company properly, she liked the idea of not having an overgrown twelve-year-old burning carelessly through a hundred and twenty millions dollars in investment, but there was something about Bernard . . .

And she had an itchy feeling that down deep there was still something she did not understand.

Bernard at least hadn't tried to make her eat a hot dog made of bean curd.

His hot dogs had been made of questionable meat by-products, chemically created cheese filling, and jalapeño peppers specially imported from Mexico.

Whereas a hot dog made from tofu is like champagne made from Pepto Bismol.

"I talked to Bernard, and he was not, exactly, forthcoming. So I called Chen Li in Beijing tonight."

"And?"

"As far as he knows, everything they've been doing is for the new 'Murder Mystery' game."

"And is it?"

"No. At least not the game we've been given proposals on. All the modeling our China team is doing is of Bernard's neighborhood."

"You mean of Bernard's murder!"

"Uh, I would assume. We're going to have to ask him that question tomorrow."

Johannsen looked furious. "We're going to have to do a lot more than that tomorrow. You and I are going to drive out there, and I'm going to need you to locate here in the Bay Area for an indefinite time. I'm going to need a new CEO I can trust to clean up this mess."

"I don't know what to say."

Johannsen's face was turning redder by the minute. "There's nothing *to* say. I'm sorry, Kelly, you'll have to forgive me. I'm going to have to leave early." He called to a waitress. "Excuse me, can you put this in a box and get a check for me? I have an emergency I need to attend to."

Then to Kelly: "I have to make a few phone calls to prepare for tomorrow. I'll call you tomorrow morning at your hotel to give you my plans."

With that Johannsen got up and walked to the counter to pay the bill, stopping briefly to whisper something into a customer's ear. Kelly noticed that the customer he talked to quickly pulled out an iPhone and began typing something.

Kelly's heart had dropped. Had she just hammered a final nail into Bernard's career coffin? Had she just been named CEO of a company with over a hundred million dollars in funding?

The daze of these questions left her briefly as she realized she had just been spared the need to eat a tofu and goat cheese hot dog on a slice of whole-wheat sourdough french bread.

The comforting thought was quickly replaced by the realization that she would be relocating to Northern California "indefinitely," which could mean daily tofu dogs with Johannsen for some time to come.

12

(Select) *A narrow slice of beach, then Limei's house and the pigeon coop, are highlighted within a bordered 3-D cube.*

(Copy) *The cube becomes a shade darker.*

(Paste) *A copy of the cube jolts into being just north of the darkened selection, shoving the rest of the world farther north.*

(Paste) *Another copy pops into existence, knocking the first and the world beyond yet farther north. (Paste) And another. (Paste, paste, paste . . .) More sections pop the earlier ones yet farther north . . .*

(Paste, paste, paste, paste . . .) *The thin slice of beach continuously duplicates northward into the distance like a rogue tectonic plate on tequila and Red Bull, wreaking havoc on the previously clean modeling that had so exactly connected sections of reality along the beachfront of Cliff Shores.*

And, behold, suddenly a seemingly unending string of the rectangular slices comprising beach, beach house, and pigeon coop line up neatly along the shoreline.

Lester Argyle wonders briefly over the regional devastation a brick-and-mortar disturbance of this sort in the tectonic plate would cause. A select stretch of the region's entire coast would have suddenly jumped several miles to the north.

Looking down . . .

"Let's open a square here," the voice of Lester Argyle echoes in the sky. *"Yes, here . . . Good. OK, leave the default settings on for wind, go with full earth gravity, and just drop one. See what happens."*

A black square opens a hundred yards in the sky above the first slice of beach and a second later an oversize man falls through it, arms and legs fluttering wildly, and plummets down onto the pigeon coop. The collision thoroughly smashes the structure into a pile of lumber and splinters and sends blood everywhere.

*In video games, spurting blood is a lot like cars blowing up on TV;
blood and fiery wrecks sell better than reality.*

"Yyyyiiikkkeeess . . ." *Les says with a disappointed tone.*

"Let me try," *Eric Lyle insists, and a hole opens over the next
stretch, this one a little lower in the sky, and this time a dead body
plummets upside down and smashes into the coop, destroying it
completely.*

"Try it with some wind," *Les says, and a hole opens just east of
the third slice. This time the man sails down at an angle and smashes
into the side of the beach house, sending blood everywhere.*

"Oh heck," *Les says, "fire at will."*

*And for the next twenty minutes heavy-set murder victims come
raining down onto the succession of beach houses for miles along the
coast, smashing into the coop, the houses, and the street below in a
sick and virtually unprecedented weather pattern that completely
fails to set the victim in any way onto an unbroken pigeon loft.*

🎮 🎮 🎮

It had not been a pleasant flight in any way.

Kramer had been so angry at finding Chief O'Brian in the hotel
bar ducking his calls—in concert with that crazy resort manager
who was extorting the both of them—that he insisted on flying
out that afternoon, even though the resulting itinerary put them
into San Francisco later than if they had waited till the following
morning to depart.

After flying from Maui they wound up twice having to change
planes between Honolulu and San Francisco, a situation O'Brian
found particularly disturbing since he couldn't think of any land
on which to stop between the two cities, which are separated by
roughly half the Pacific Ocean.

They flew first on a red-eye with too much turbulence and too
little leg room to allow for sleeping, bringing them to Vancouver,
where they had a four-hour layover, and a few hours after taking
off from there they passed agonizingly *over* San Francisco ("if
you look out the left side of the aircraft you can see downtown

San Francisco . . .") and a while after that landed at Los Angeles International Airport, where they waited two hours before boarding a flight that brought them back to San Francisco.

Salt in the wound for O'Brian, Kramer bought coach tickets, meaning bad food, bad seats, a bad back, and all with the knowledge that the return leg of the expensive business-class ticket O'Brian had bought for his vacation would go to waste—well, or make his wife, who had stayed behind, doubly comfy upon her return, with two business-class seats to herself.

O'Brian breathed a sigh of relief as they walked off the plane and into the gate, thinking the worst was over—only to find that it was not: Waiting for them there at the gate stood Mayor Dennings and he did not look the very picture of happiness.

"This is not how I like to spend my Saturdays," he said angrily as he approached O'Brian and Kramer.

An unpleasant conversation ensued in which O'Brian sang the praises of the county police and the technology that allowed him to stay on top of the investigation from Maui, and even guide it (well, in spirit, while sipping drinks with little umbrellas in them), and in which Mayor Dennings trashed the county police and gave a discourse on the virtues of community centers and ballroom dancing, both of which the residents of Cliff Shores were at risk of losing because of their police chief's negligence.

Kramer for his part found it prudent to remain quiet, nodding occasionally on the mention of ballrooms, but otherwise letting the mayor vent on the police chief the anger he had been directing at Kramer all this time.

But if O'Brian thought the worst had come and gone with the mayor's appearance at the gate, he was far from correct, for a half an hour later he found himself crammed with all his luggage in the backseat of the mayor's two-door BMW as they sped off to Cliff Shores where the police chief was damned well, the mayor insisted, going to take over the investigation and make an arrest— that very day, if possible.

Heading in the same direction on the same freeway were Lester Argyle and his design team. They were on their way to Bernard's to discuss what other features they might add to the game.

Les was crawling along at a pace agonizingly slow for the drivers around him, explaining as they proceeded how maintaining a certain motion and speed in a Prius improved its gas mileage. A diagram on the dashboard video screen made it a graphic presentation.

What it failed to display was how infuriated the drivers behind him became as he inched along, slowing, then speeding, all with neither brake lights nor apparent reason.

Inside the car, the three passengers were engulfed in laptops, and even Les, who was driving, was wearing Bluetooth headphones that picked up music from his dash-mounted MP3 player and comparing, as they drove, three GPS navigation systems—the in-dash navigator, a navigation device mounted on the windshield, and the one on his Android phone.

Occasionally he also leaned over and watched the laptop Eric Lyle was using in the passenger seat beside him, commenting on how he should do this or that as Eric matched his skills at "Alien Invasion" against the passengers in the rear seat, who sat a few feet apart but were passing the game data to one another via satellite.

It was an unlikely cavalry racing (slowly) down the freeway to Bernard's and Limei's rescue.

🎮 🎮 🎮

Sergeant Bill Peterson looked at the four files on his desk. One was for the parking dispute; one was for some dead baby birds that had been found, apparently abandoned by their parents on North Cliff; one was a complaint about excessive noise from the Beachfront Café; and one was for the murder investigation.

Nervously he picked up and opened the last, sipping Alka-Seltzer Plus as he read.

This was not why Peterson had become a police officer.

He had talked to the police chief on the phone moments before and he sincerely wished he had not become a police officer.

O'Brian's connection wasn't clear. The chief seemed to be on the road and he sounded extremely angry. He muttered something about being crammed in a car and he shouted a good five minutes of orders before hanging up.

The main door opened and Peterson watched as Captain Dirk Toland entered.

Toland had a swagger in his step as he made his way into the office section of the station.

He was going to arrest someone today. This was why Toland had become a police officer.

"Let's go, Peterson," he said. "We're gonna arrest us a murder suspect today."

"No, I'm afraid we're not, at least not by ourselves." Peterson said weakly, the boldest statement he had ever put forth to Toland. But it was not boldness so much as his being overcome by terror.

"What do you mean? I've outlined the evidence. We may not get a conviction but we'll be able to say we solved the case."

"Chief O'Brian just called. He's back in town and is taking charge of the case. Said he wanted to meet you and me over at the Wangs' house at one p.m."

"Chief O'Brian?"

"Yep. The case is back in Cliff Shores' hands, but O'Brian said he talked to the county and was told you would be assigned to assist."

"What?! But I'm in charge . . ." Toland had seen six missed calls on his cell phone, which he normally kept on silent, and with the anticipation of getting to arrest a murder suspect had ignored them.

"Not anymore. The chief ordered us to be there at one."

"*Your* chief doesn't get to order *me*," Toland said, opening his phone and hitting Call History.

All six calls were from his department.

He checked Text Messages and saw that he had one. Quickly he fumbled to read it.

And the swagger quickly was sucked out of his demeanor as he read.

"Stop all current work on the Cliff Shores investigation," it said. "Proceed with Sergeant Peterson and report to Chief O'Brian immediately."

"Shit," Toland said, and read on:

"And turn on your goddamned ringer, Toland!" it said.

"Double shit."

🐦 🐦 🐦

Kelly Chambers was not as enthusiastic about green-vehicle technology as were the game designers.

Kelly was riding along the freeway at fifty miles an hour with George Johannsen in a car the size of a golf cart, and probably a lot less sturdy, she judged.

Scrunched in a backseat was Omar Crenshaw, another investor in OffCide Studios and a member of the board. His face was even paler than Kelly's.

"It's electric!" Johannsen had exclaimed excitedly as they pulled onto Highway 101—a wide freeway as it passes San Francisco—their windows wide open. "I charge it in my garage!"

An eighteen-wheeler zipped by them dangerously close on the right, rocking the tiny vehicle as it passed.

"I paid a hundred and twenty thousand dollars for it!"

He was shouting because both the windows and the "moon roof," as he called it, were wide open, making it nearly impossible to hear.

"She goes up to fifty-five, but I like to keep her under fifty."

They were moving at a snail's crawl by California standards, with cars whipping by in threatening ways, leaving a look of terror on Kelly's and Crenshaw's faces.

Making matters worse, Johannsen was switching lanes and weaving between vehicles, forcing other cars to slow suddenly and in a few cases nearly crash.

"Now *this* is good for the environment!" Johannsen shouted.

They were on their way to Bernard's studio for a showdown, an event Kelly was not looking forward to. She quickly found herself getting carsick, the taste of the whole-grain waffles and soy milk Johannsen had forced her to eat at breakfast mixing in her throat.

Soy milk.

Kelly hadn't been aware even that soy beans were mammals and mused briefly over the notion. The musing stopped when the taste solidified in her mouth.

"I'll be interested to see this *studio* that Walker spent so much of his money on—and getting an explanation of why he's been spending so much *company* money on worthless animation!" Joannsen shouted over the wind storm.

Kelly was terrified enough by California freeways, which were wider than any she knew back east, and far faster—that is, on Saturdays. On Monday to Friday they typically were at a standstill all day, with the afternoon rush hour beginning slightly after the noon rush hour, which itself pretty much followed the morning commute time. Kelly really couldn't understand how people tolerated the freeway lifestyle.

And she had spent much of the previous night awake in bed worrying that if Johannsen fired or demoted Bernard and made her CEO, she would have to remain in this hateful land of gourmet health food (she hadn't seen real butter in days!), green vehicles, and epic freeways.

She took out an antacid and chewed it down, nearly choking on it as Johannsen skipped two lanes to squeeze between a big rig and a Winnebago.

🐾 🐾 🐾

"They're going to arrest your grandfather today," Francine said with a stern look on her face. This was the sort of issue that had inspired Francine to become a social worker: real-world problems that people faced. Only now, in the face of a real problem, it didn't seem all that inspirational.

Limei looked up at Francine sadly, her grandparents behind her wondering what was going on.

"Captain Toland called me this morning and said I had better drive down."

Francine broke into Chinese and explained to the grandparents.

By the time she finished Limei was running around shoving items into a grocery bag—a half a loaf of bread, a box of cereal, her grandfather's medicines . . .

"Women yao zou (we have to go)," she kept repeating.

"I have our organization's attorney coming down," Francine told her. "The best thing for us to do now is to cooperate."

But Limei ignored her.

"Women qu duimian! (we're going across the street)," she told her grandfather as she shoved several bottles of mineral water into the bag.

Her grandmother tried to take command of the situation, insisted that Limei calm down. Her grandfather stood by bravely and tried to calm her.

But five minutes later Limei was leading him by the arm across the street and up the outer stairs to Bernard's studio, with Francine in tow, her grandmother standing in the doorway watching in disbelief.

🕊 🕊 🕊

Bernard had slept until ten Saturday morning, having been up much of the night videoconferencing with Lester Argyle—one of the few people Bernard felt had any true competence with games.

Earlier Bernard had installed the final modeling on the greater neighborhood, from the highway behind to the ocean, and along the beach from the small cliffs in the north to the rocky jetty in the south.

In the past few weeks they had assembled a 3-D model of everything right down to shop signs, parking spaces, and trees, and it was a model that players' avatars could walk through and interact with, including murdering one another and hanging bodies from pigeon coops.

What's more, at least seven game designers locally and in Beijing had played the program, which was more reality than it was game, and approached the murder from every conceivable angle, as murderer, as victim, and as police officer.

No plausible explanation had been found.

Bernard went back over all of this with Argyle using shared desktops.

Argyle had been in on some of the groundbreaking reality games, games that contained larger stories and universes that characters maneuvered in. He was the one who showed Bernard that these went well beyond games; they were art, they were literature, they were imagination.

Now Bernard was trying to use them to understand the circumstances surrounding a murder, and for the first time since he had entered the "Death World 3: Plunderer of Societies" World Championship when he was in the eleventh grade, for the first time since then he felt unsure of himself.

What he needed to find, Lester told him now, was a bridge from the modeling to reality.

"What was there that night that is *not* in our modeling?"

"What do you mean?"

"Our modeling lets you examine not *everything*, but only the things that were there during our photo and video shoots. What else was there that night?"

"I cannot go back in time and *re*-shoot!" Bernard said grandly. "If I could do that, this whole business would be concluded. Limei's grandfather would be out of trouble and that cursed pigeon coop would be gone for good."

"But you *have* to go back in time—that's *exactly* what you have to do."

"And how do you suggest I do that?"

"Think horizontally. You're thinking only vertically."

"Blah, blah, blah . . ." Bernard responded.

"I'm serious. Your modeling might be forcing you *not* to see things, since obviously there is *something* or some *things* that are not in it."

"I need a sandwich," Bernard said.

Bernard went on to sit up late into the night—over pastrami and cheese, microwavable burritos, and Pepsi—contemplating the models and trying to see what possibly could be missing.

He thought of all the impressions he had taken in of the neighborhood—people walking, birds scavenging along the beach, joggers, surfers, elderly folks walking their dogs in the evenings . . .

What had been there on that fateful Saturday night that did not show in his game?

He went to sleep with the haunting feeling that time was running out . . .

🐦 🐦 🐦

. . . and spent the morning sitting at his desk with the modeling on the five large TV screens around him, the doors and windows open to let in the real sounds, smells, and sights of Cliff Shores.

Gulls were scavenging along the beach as they did every day, hoping more for tossed french fries than the bounty nature provided.

Several teenagers were using one end of the public parking lot as a skateboard park.

Three surfers were donning wetsuits as they prepared to try out the cold waves, while at the far end of the beach, a man was more or less failing in his attempts to wind-surf.

And out in the distance the sight of a yacht was growing larger as it headed in toward shore.

🐦 🐦 🐦

Limei led her grandfather up the outside stairs to Bernard's studio getting much the same resistance one is likely to meet when dragging a dog into a bath. But when she got him to the door he forgot all that was going on and looked around in wonder, and with a new respect for his strange neighbor.

Her grandfather looked around the room in amazement—the life-size statues of women (especially the one who wore buns on either ear); the pinball machine; the half circle of huge flat-screen TVs, each displaying scenes he recognized from around the neighborhood; the U-shaped desk with several computers about it; the thronelike lounge chair next to the window where he knew Bernard slept; and not least of all Bernard himself, seated at the desk surrounded by sandwiches (with one in each hand!), open bags of potato chips, and a huge cup of some drink.

Bernard was equally startled. Though he had been working feverishly to help Limei's grandfather, he still believed his neighbor was out to kill him because of the pigeon coop. He never expected to see him in the studio.

But Bernard's surprise was quickly overcome by the sight of tears in Limei's eyes.

"The police are coming to arrest Grandfather!" she said. "Francine is downstairs. They called her this morning. It's that turkey, Captain Toland."

"Oh no . . ."

"You have to hide us."

"What?"

"You have to hide us. Maybe in one of your closets."

"Believe me, you are too young, and your grandfather too old, to survive the sight of one of my closets. You can't hide him here."

"Why not?"

"You'll get us all arrested."

"But you have to help us."

The whole conversation was interrupted by the sight of Lester Argyle and the development team on the outside stairwell.

"Knock knock," Argyle said and opened the door himself. The four came in and as if they had practiced their entry, quickly helped themselves to bits of Bernard's desk where each opened a laptop.

Limei's grandfather looked on, even more bewildered.

Argyle cleared away an area of sandwiches and chips next to Bernard, opened his laptop, and produced three cups of Starbucks coffee.

"I'm going to download a new video graphic of the pigeon hut," he said.

"*Coop.*" Bernard shot back. "*Pizza* is sold in huts. Pizza Huts. *Pigeons* are kept in *coops*." Bernard said.

"Actually *lofts*, to be correct," Argyle said. "Pigeon *lofts*. I looked it up on Wikipedia."

"Wikipedia has an entry on pigeon coops?" Bernard asked.

"Wikipedia has an entry on the anatomy of toenails," Lester assured him.

"Some people have entirely too much time on their hands. And clearly I pay you too much." Bernard said. "Do you look up things like this on company time?"

"No. I use company time to help solve unauthorized murder investigations."

"Fair point."

"Now, let me show you what I've put together."

"Bernard . . ." Limei pleaded, trying to regain his attention, but before he answered, three more figures appeared on the landing outside, three figures very interested in the unauthorized use of company time for murder investigations: George Johannsen, Kelly Chambers, and Omar Crenshaw.

As Argyle had, Johannsen opened the door without asking and led his party in. He proceeded to inspect the room with a perplexed expression: the Star Wars statues, the pinball machine, posters of science fiction movies covering the walls, the absurd wooden structure across the alley—but most of all, the video screens.

"Uh-huh?" he said finally. "Walker! You have wasted company money on personal business," he said in a tone nearly as cutting as his stare.

Bernard took on a more-bloated look than usual. "I would have you know, I have invested a conservative amount of our R&D budget on research and development," he countered tensely, picking up a meatball sandwich in one hand and a potato chip in the other.

"And what have you researched?! A police investigation you were warned not to get involved in, a murder investigation, in fact, that you are a person of interest in—the police have stated that publicly, which is real great for our company image, I'll add."

Bernard fumbled around his desk for a Snickers bar, finally found one.

Johannsen stepped forward, his face growing more serious.

Argyle looked at Bernard, at the candy bar. Limei looked at Bernard. Eric Lyle, incredibly, turned his attention away from his video game console to look at Bernard.

"Walker, I think it is fair for you to assume that you are fire—"

But before Johannsen could complete his sentence, the door again swung open, this time revealing Chief O'Brian, followed by Mayor Dennings, City Manager Orland Kramer, Captain Toland, Sergeant Peterson, and rearmost, Francine, who was standing on her tiptoes trying to see over the crowd.

Incredibly, they all managed somehow to squeeze in, making the room, which normally seemed large, uncomfortably cramped, and probably breaking city codes for maximum occupancy in the process.

"This is him?" O'Brian asked Toland, indicating Limei's grandfather.

"That's him," Toland replied.

"You, sir, are under arrest," O'Brian proclaimed.

"What?!" Bernard demanded.

"This is the video game guy?" O'Brian asked Toland.

"*This* is Mr. Walker, Chief O'Brian," the mayor interjected. "Mr. Walker is graciously helping us to build our new community center, you will remember."

"Yes, well, Mr. Walker was told not to meddle in this investigation."

"I'm not sure who you are," Bernard countered, "but there has been no credible murder investigation so far other than the one I have carried out—at considerable expense to myself and my company, I might add." He shot a look to Johannsen as he said it.

"And I can assure you," Bernard went on, "that this gentleman did *not* commit—*could not have* committed—the murder. And I can prove it."

"Oh yeah? And how's that?" O'Brian challenged.

Bernard pressed several buttons on a keyboard in front of him and the five large screens began panning different areas of the neighborhood: one, the alley below, between the two houses;

another the beach; another the highway above; and two others streets between.

The crowded room uncomfortably shifted until everyone could see the screens, mouths open at the wonder. The neighborhood they had all just passed through to get to Bernard's was now surrounding them indoors, in high-definition graphics.

"My god . . ." O'Brian muttered.

The same thought went through Johannsen's head.

"What you are seeing," Bernard explained grandly, "is thorough and accurate modeling of the entire town, right down to the rocks along the side of the beach path. And the people you see are all Cliff Shores residents—look, there's Limei, and there I am. And over on that screen is the murder victim."

O'Brian's mouth opened even wider.

"And I can play—and several of our engineers and China development team already have played—the part of the different characters you see here. We can navigate through this virtual Cliff Shores and try to murder the victim and hang him on the pigeon coop."

He saw he had the full attention of everyone.

"Among the detail we have added is the number of nails and all the materials used in constructing the coop. And one thing we have ascertained beyond doubt is that this gentleman, and for that matter no one on the ground, could possibly have hung the victim on that coop."

"What the hell are you talking about?" O'Brian demanded.

"What's the name of that graphic, Les?"

"Loft."

"What?"

"Loft—L-O-F-T, as in pigeon loft. Remember."

"Coop," Bernard corrected as he hit another few buttons, while taking another bite of the meatball sandwich. And on the central screen a graphic of Limei's house and the pigeon loft appeared.

Lester Argyle took over.

"We inspected the rooftop structure and discovered its construction to be far from up to standard." He leaned in and pushed a few buttons, causing red circles to appear at key spots on the loft.

"We identified nine different points on this side of the loft—where the victim was found—that are connected with nails far too short for their intended purpose."

"And the fact of the matter is," Bernard interjected, "that the victim could not possibly have been placed there from the ground or from this house or the one across the street without the entire structure being pulled to the ground by the weight. The victim had to have been placed—very carefully placed—there, from above."

All faces turned to study the graph, leaving the room in silence for several seconds.

Then O'Brian exploded: "From the air? What, are you saying the victim was dropped from an airplane? Are you nuts?"

"I believe he is," Johannsen put in.

The mayor jumped in again. "Now, we do have to be grateful to Mr. Walker for the effort he has put forward in aid of our city," he said.

"No," Bernard answered. "I'm afraid the victim could not have been dropped from an airplane. The velocity and falling weight would have torn the structure apart."

"So what, then, are you proposing that someone flew a helicopter to put the body there? That would be an awful lot of trouble when the murderer would have been better off dropping the body into the sea." O'Brian said.

"That is a problem regardless of how the body got there—the *why*. But, no, it could not have been a helicopter. I was asleep right over there. A helicopter would have woken me up."

"So just how the hell do you explain the body getting up there? Because if you don't have anything more than some crazy theory, I'm going to stick this man in jail. The county has concluded that he is the prime suspect."

"Yes," Johannsen joined in. "I'd like to ask that same question. After squandering away all of this money, just how do you explain this?"

Bernard in his father's view had wasted his life away on video games and now Bernard was faced with a moment of truth: a moment that could very well prove his father, and prove George Johannsen, correct, and make him look like a fool in front of all these people. He also noticed suddenly that Francine Lin was in the room.

Or it could be a moment that would make him shine, that would offer tremendous and final vindication.

It was the moment for action; all eyes were on Bernard now, expecting that action.

Standing before the group, Bernard looked down to the laptop in front of him and opened a game called "KittyRanch: The Great Escape" (that allows players to be little kittens trying to escape a kitty cattle drive, or to be kitty-cowboys trying to keep the kittens in line). And with everyone staring, speechless, Bernard proceeded to gently guide two straying kittens back into the kitty herd, his hand shivering on the mouse, sweat stains on his shirt now growing visible beyond his vest.

Bernard looked up and glared out the window, as if about to say something profound. The room somehow managed to grow tenser.

He typed again into the laptop, setting it to record an episode of the Japanese cartoon "Naruto."

"Naruto" played on Saturdays. This was a Saturday.

Returning his gaze to the window, Bernard tried to think. What had they missed in their modeling?!

"Naruto" . . . Saturday . . .

Les and the team had never been out to film on a Saturday, on a weekend. They had never imaged the streets on a Saturday, had never filmed the area or done a photo shoot on a Saturday.

Was there something different about Saturdays, Bernard wondered, his gaze still on the window?

And as quickly as these questions shot through his mind, he realized he was looking directly at the answer.

Off to the right the hang gliders were back, as they were most weekend days, hovering above the water near North Cliff.

A shot of adrenaline shot up Bernard's spine and hit his brain.

13

Looking down at the spot where the waves hit the rocks below, Damian Howard Mitchell basked in the adrenaline he always experienced when hang gliding along the cliffs.

First out, then down, gaining speed, then up to a slow bend, up more . . .

He swooped out, and, leaning to his left, made a long lofty turn back toward the hills, then hung there. From the ground it seemed as if he weren't moving at all, and in fact he hardly was.

Down along the cliff, several birds huddled to protect their nests from the menacing hang gliders, to them seemingly large birds invading their air space.

Damian made the same move twice more, the second time having to dodge one of the birds as it shot out at him in defense.

Damian smiled. These birds once had been a serious threat, a threat to the sport he loved and his favorite hang gliding cliff. That was no longer the case.

🎮 🎮 🎮

"Hang gliders?!" O'Brian practically shouted. "You're trying to tell me the victim was hung by a hang glider? You're crazy, completely crazy."

Bernard thought for a moment.

"Give me forty-eight hours. Come back here Monday afternoon and I will have a full explanation for you. I will have all the evidence to prove it."

"I will *not* come back Monday," O'Brian insisted. "I came here to make an arrest and an arrest I am going to make."

The mayor stepped forward. "I don't think so, Ron. Mr. Walker is a distinguished member of our community, and as such, he should be given the benefit of the doubt. This case has been left hanging long enough while you were gallivanting around the beaches of Hawaii. It can last another weekend."

"Seriously? You're going to buy this?"

"Yes, Chief, I am. Let's give Mr. Walker the two days he's asking for and see what he comes up with. I think we should err on the side of *not* making a false arrest of an elderly Cliff Shores homeowner."

"What?!" O'Brian asked, astounded, thinking of how he had ended his vacation and spent an eternity on an airplane—for this.

Fuming, he looked at Limei's grandfather.

"Listen, you will *not* leave Cliff Shores between now and Monday afternoon."

"Cliff Shows?" Limei's grandfather asked. He hadn't understood a word anyone had said, but at one point he was quite sure they were commending him on the construction of his pigeon coop, with the graph of it showing on the screen.

Francine stepped forward and interpreted. "Ta shuo zhe liang tian ni bukeyi likai Cliff Shores. Ni liaojie mo?"

He nodded his head. "Liaojie (understand) . . ."

Moments later, as she led Lao Wang out, Francine explained to him what had transpired.

O'Brian stormed out with Toland following. Peterson followed the mayor and the city manager.

As for Johannsen, he stopped in front of Bernard before departing. "Even if you come up with something on this, you are still *so* fired. Finished!"

Bernard fumbled about in his pockets for something to eat.

"And I'll be back here Monday afternoon, too. I want to see first-hand just what it is you have done. And I'll be bringing the full board with me, along with a careful succession plan for *your* job. Come," he commanded to Kelly and Crenshaw, and headed for the door.

"Wait," Kelly said. She looked over at Argyle. "Can you give me a lift back into San Francisco in a while?"

"You bet," Les said cheerfully. Les was a twenty-four-year-old kid who spent sixteen hours a day playing video games. He didn't often have women asking him for rides somewhere.

Kelly looked at Johannsen. "I think I'd better stay here long enough to inventory the computer files that company time and money were spent creating."

"Good thinking," Johannsen said to Kelly, grateful at her confidence in taking charge. "I'll talk to you later by phone." And with that he and Crenshaw left.

Once they were out of sight, Kelly turned to Bernard.

"Two questions. One, are you sure you can prove this hang glider business?" she asked.

"Beyond doubt," Bernard answered, as if offended at the question. "And your second question?"

"Can you take me back to that minimart? I could sure use one of those hot dogs."

"I would welcome the trip. My lunch here has been totally ruined," he said, gesturing to the sandwiches and chips that now had been pushed about by the engineers. "You'd think people could wait until *after* lunch before launching into arrest fits and the like."

"I will agree with that," Kelly said. "Also, I couldn't bear the thought of riding back into town in that death trap of an electric car that Johannsen paid a small fortune for." And to Argyle: "And thank *you* for the ride," she said with a look of relief on her face.

"No prob', but you'll have to cram into the backseat of my Prius with these two," he said indicating his colleagues.

"Damn."

🐦 🐦 🐦

An hour later, Bernard stood alone gazing out at his studio's view—with a smile for the first time since the night he had moved in.

Off around North Cliff, several hang gliders swooped out over the water, occasionally sparring for air space with one or two birds that appeared to nest along the rock walls.

After a discussion of how a hang glider might have been used, Bernard had assigned the engineers to plan some additional modeling, then sent them off, with a frowning Kelly crammed in the back of Les's Prius.

And now Bernard was startled suddenly to see Limei standing silently outside at the top of the stairs. He opened the glass door.

"And what, may I ask, are you doing standing there like that?"

"I'm scared," she said.

"Why? As I said, I have found the answer to this big puzzle the police have failed to look at properly."

"Uh, no offense, Bernard, but I explained it again to my grandfather and he turned white. He said you're crazy, and to be honest, it sounds a little like you are."

"What?! I am offended. Here I have risked my career, and you show no gratitude?!" Bernard nervously took a Mars bar out of his shirt pocket.

Limei looked at him with a begging expression, "But . . . but how could a *hang glider* carry a body?"

"Ah," Bernard said, an air of superiority lighting up his face. "We are putting together new modeling to determine just that."

Limei looked even more doubtful. "No way! One hang glider's going to carry two people, one of them the big dead guy? You're crazy."

"Ah, but do a quick image search on "hang glider" and look what you get." Bernard quickly spun a laptop around and did a search. The screen filled with hang gliders.

"Yeah . . ." Limei challenged.

Now he added "two people" to the search and the results showed several hang gliders configured for two passengers.

"Hmm . . ." Limei said.

"And watch what you get when you change the search to *motorized* hang glider." He did so and now the screen filled with an assortment of improbable vehicles, with hang gliders attached to everything from a boat with wheels to a spacesuit.

"It turns out that there are *motorized* hang gliders, *machine driven*—primarily by crazy people, no doubt—but motorized hang gliders that could likely handle a heavy load with some consistency. We'll get real specs and test weights and numbers with our new modeling."

"But how could you ever prove something so crazy? Even if you're right, the murderer is probably long gone and took his hang glider with him."

"But just maybe we *can* find the hang glider."

"What do you mean?"

"There's a chance we can find the hang glider if we can find *what?*"

Limei looked confused.

"Listen," Bernard said, "you're overlooking one essential question: Why would the murderer want to leave the body on your grandfather's pigeon coop?"

"I can't imagine why. And if we can't even answer that, you're not going to prove he put it there with a hang glider."

"Ah, but you see, that's just it: I am guessing the murderer did *not* intend to hang the body there. Why would he? If you were going to hang a body from a hang glider and drop it somewhere, would you lay it out crucified on a pigeon coop? Or maybe try to take it somewhere where it would never be found."

"You mean like the ocean?"

"Uh-huh. I am guessing that the ocean was the target and that the pigeon coop got in the way. And if that's the case, we might get some idea of what happened to the hang glider if we can find *what?*"

Now Limei was completely lost. "What?"

"The victim's missing shoe," Bernard said, raising an eyebrow.

Minutes later they were on the beach scouring their way toward the water.

Cliff Shores' main beach was a pristine stretch of white sand— void of litter or remnants of beach fires, or anything else that nature itself did not wash ashore.

A shoe would have stood out clearly from the grainy sand. The bright yellow shoe in question might well have been visible from outer space.

"If we can find it," Bernard explained, "its location may point to some answers. Literally."

"But it's been too long. A shoe would have been picked up and thrown away, or washed away by the tide."

"We have to look anyway." Bernard was forcing himself to remain optimistic, knowing the shoe was about the only solid clue they had to grasp onto.

The two of them spread out, heads down to the sand, walking in zigzags.

Bernard stopped frequently to dig at the sand with his foot, wondering if a shoe could get buried in that amount of time.

Limei stopped at one point and pulled on something yellow and slimy that was stuck under a rock, but only to reveal a bit of seaweed that Bernard would not have dared touch.

They had covered a wide area over more than half an hour when Bernard stopped to tie his shoe. He eyed Limei's house, only about twenty feet away, wondering how far the yellow shoe could have traveled. And then found out, as he spotted it deep in a bush right next to him.

"Ah-hah!" he said, standing.

Limei came running, stood beside him, and followed his gaze into the bush. There she saw, lying quietly on its side, the absurdly bright-yellow Nike sneaker.

Bernard leaned down to get a closer view, then looked at the beach house and beyond. From this perspective, he realized, he was looking at more of the crime than anyone had been able to fathom thus far.

He then produced an iPhone and snapped several photos of the shoe, then of Limei's house from where they stood.

"Aren't you going to pick it up and look at it?" Limei asked.

"No. The police will want it untouched. It's evidence. Of course, by the time they get around to looking at it, I will have already figured everything out. But we have to make the police feel important. I'll send these photos to Peterson from my phone."

"And this shoe will somehow tell you what happened to the hang glider?"

Bernard looked at her, turned again to face her grandparents' house, then the shoe again. And then he looked out to the water.

"Yes," he said.

🐦 🐦 🐦

City Manager Orland Kramer was not overly surprised to find Mayor Ted Dennings on the front step when he opened the door.

Dennings started off without a greeting: "I want you to instruct Chief O'Brian to assign the entire police force to help Walker. Hire off-duty officers from the county if you have to."

"Are you serious? They're not going to find anything. That Walker is out of his mind. There's no way someone on a hang glider somehow got that body onto that roof."

"I know, and I don't care. He was about one step away from formally promising a grant to the city for the new community center, and this murder business has set him back *several* steps. I want him *to know* that this city is one hundred percent behind him now, even if he says *fairies* put the body there."

"O'Brian is not happy about all this. He thinks we should have arrested the Wang guy today."

"O'Brian is about two steps away from job-hunting. Let him know that, and tell him if the community center funding doesn't come through, I'm going to blame it on his goddamned Hawaiian vacation."

Kramer had seen in previous city jobs how some mayors and city council members could miraculously go from cultured, respectable, seemingly ethical people, to conniving politicians in an flash. Not all of them, but some.

"What do you hope to accomplish with this? A week from now we'll still be nowhere on the case, and that abomination of a pigeon loft will still be up there posing a threat to the community and keeping Walker from funding your community center. And sooner or later we're still going to have to make an arrest in the case."

"And what's worse," Kramer continued, "it has dawned on me that the police have focused on the elderly neighbor out of convenience more than out of actual *evidence*, of which there isn't any."

"So what's your point?"

"O'Brian or the county could suddenly decide that *Walker* is the better suspect. We could very well find your would-be benefactor is the county's would-be scapegoat in the case."

"As I said, O'Brian will work with us, or he'll be working somewhere *other* than Cliff Shores. So let's make a show of force for Walker. I want a squad car parked on the alley where Walker can see it twenty-four seven. I want all officers right down to our meter maid searching the area for more evidence—*hang glider* evidence. And I want you personally to visit Walker and ask him what we the city and what our police force can do for him as he furthers his investigation. Got all of that?"

"OK..."

Kramer saw that Cliff Shores' powerless mayor turned out in fact to have a fair deal of power.

"And let's make sure we're all there on Monday afternoon to hear what Walker has to say, and I want to see you *and* O'Brian backing him up all the way—I don't care if he says a goddamned UFO put the body up there. Got that?"

"Got it."

🐦 🐦 🐦

"We have two research subs here at the institute," the woman was explaining to a small crowd before her. Dr. Alisha Sharma, director of the Cliff Shores Institute for Oceanic Research, was tall and slim and wore straight black hair that fell onto her white lab coat. She had pronounced facial features with a bare hint of wrinkle under her eyes.

"The one you see here has a cagelike structure attached to the front. That is used for mapping and other tasks. The sub itself holds three people and can be used for a variety of research.

"Tragically," she added with an elegant accent, "its condition is such that we have been forced to ground it, and we have been told it cannot be retrofitted. This has left us only with this other, tiny two-person sub, which cannot do what we need it to. The situation is such that it has put much of our research here at the institute at a virtual standstill.

"Worse, in this economy we've been unable to secure new federal or state funding. In fact we have *lost* a good deal of funding.

And even private sources have dried up—and *dry up* is not a phrasal verb you want to hear when your job is oceanic research.

"Now, before we move on indoors to the aquarium, does anyone have any questions?"

An elderly woman at the front spoke out: "How deep do these submarines go?"

"The larger sub can be used safely in waters as deep as three hundred meters and still have reliable maneuverability."

"Wouldn't it be very uncomfortable when crammed with three people?" a man asked.

Sharma smiled. "Let's just say it's an unwritten rule that everyone bathes well before each trip."

This got a chuckle from the tour group; it was a line Sharma used a lot.

Then a voice from the back: "How deep does the smaller sub go?"

Here the researcher lost her smile. She clearly was not interested in speaking about the smaller vessel.

"The smaller one is good only in much-shallower waters, and it does not have independent maneuverability. It is dependent on being attached to a research vessel at the surface. But if you'll look at the larger sub—"

The voice interrupted her. "But the smaller one *is* working?"

"Yes. But as I explained, we have been shut down by a lack of funding needed to replace the larger unit—"

"But the small one could get, say, a few hundred yards out and down?"

"Um . . . yes." Now Sharma outright frowned. "But our entire focus at this time is trying to get the larger sub—"

"Is the smaller sub for rent?"

"What?!" Sharma said, frustrated. Whoever this unsightly man at the rear of the crowd was, he was becoming a nuisance.

"Is the smaller sub for rent?" Bernard repeated, clearly annoyed at having to repeat his question.

"No, it is *not* for rent," Sharma said. "This is an oceanic research institute, not a taxi company."

"Let me rephrase that," Bernard asked with added impatience. "How much would it take to rent it for an hour?"

"I said, it is *not* for rent. Are you part of this group, sir?"

"OK, let me put it this way: How much will it cost to replace the larger research sub?"

Sharma lost her composure completely now, but blurted out what she had said emotionally quite often lately: "Even a used replacement would run at close to five hundred thousand dollars."

She was lifting her radio to call for security as she spoke; this cretin had ruined her tour. But Bernard's reply stopped her short:

"Well, I should hope to rent the small sub for at least two hours at that price."

🐦 🐦 🐦

Five minutes later the tour group stood inside being misinformed about the aquarium's sea life, by a young volunteer intern struggling to earn extra credit at a nearby university. Dr. Sharma, meanwhile, spoke to Bernard alone in her small office.

Actually, it was more a closet than an office, and was crammed with filing cabinets and a work table overloaded with computer equipment. Bernard took special note of the filing cabinets; what did people do with filing cabinets these days? he wondered.

"Are you serious about a donation to go towards a new submarine?" Sharma asked emotionally. "Because if you aren't, please don't lead me on. I spent my entire education and career working to obtain a research post like this one, studying the California coast. Then once I arrive here, bam, the economy falls apart and I do not even receive a full salary anymore. And half of what I do get I have to put into maintenance of the aquarium—as do several other staff here."

"I see."

"I mean it. I'm here on a Saturday giving tours, as I am on Sundays, hoping against hope that a little public relations might help us. And I am busy with research the other five days of the week. I do not do all of this to have some joker come in off the street and get everyone's hopes up for new funding."

"OK, how about this? I am fully prepared to lend a hand, even if you won't rent me that small sub. But you would be doing me a great service by renting it. And you would also be helping to solve a murder."

The possibility of a new sub. The idea of renting the small sub. This strange-looking man. Not fat so much, because he was tall. Just large. Rabelais' Gargantua came to mind. And now a murder?

"OK, let's start with a little background information. Who are you and what is it that you are after?"

"My name is Bernard Walker, founder and chief executive officer of OffCide Studios, the maker of the popular video game 'Murder Mystery: The Case of the Cleavered Clerk.' "

"Uh-huh!" Sharma said. "And you need to borrow an underwater research vessel to help play a video game."

"No, I need to borrow your sub to help solve an *actual* murder. You have heard that there was a murder here in Cliff Shores a while ago, haven't you?"

Sharma's face changed. She had heard, and now that she thought about it, it all had something to do with some rich guy who ran a video game company.

"Are you for real?" she asked. "You'll have to excuse me for being skeptical."

"Very real."

"And you're willing to make a donation toward a replacement sub?"

"Fully."

"How much of the five hundred thousand I quoted for a used sub would you be prepared to contribute?"

"I would not be interested in putting good money into some *used* piece of equipment."

"Uh-huh. Well, thank you for your interest, Mr. Walker," Sharma said moving to the door. "As I said, I do not appreciate loose talk that might get our hopes up—"

"Wouldn't it make better sense if I were just to buy you a new one?" Bernard took out his iPhone and voice-dialed: "George Tanner, Attorney."

14

On Saturday evening Bernard got online with Chen Li in Beijing. With the camera too close, Chen's face filled the better part of a 50-inch flat-screen TV in Bernard's studio, an effect that was unintentional but horrid.

"George Johannsen himself called me," Chen started out. "He said you now can't ever make new assignments for our company."

"What?! Haven't we given you and your team some pretty cool jobs? If I recall, you were previously creating models promoting extermination and pest control."

Chen frowned, understanding just enough English to get Bernard's point. That is exactly what his company had assigned them before OffCide Studios came along. And the work for Bernard had been fascinating. Chen had learned more in that short time than he had in other projects at the company put together.

"Back me up and our business will stay with you—in fact, who knows, we might be looking for an acquisition. But the future's not so sure if you follow Johannsen. Most of his portfolio companies do all their outsourcing in India."

Chen took on a resigned expression.

"OK, but here it's Sunday. Our earliest to start probably will be Monday noontime."

"I need the modeling by ten Monday morning *my* time. That means you'll have to get started on it now."

"But this afternoon I have to go to a wedding banquet."

"Someone close?"

"It's my boss's daughter getting married."

"And you don't want an excuse—a *work* excuse—to miss your boss's daughter's wedding?"

Chen looked at Bernard and smiled. "So you have these hang gliders' pictures?"

🐃 🐃 🐃

Sunday morning proved to be even less pleasant for Kelly Chambers than the previous morning had. George Johannsen insisted on taking her out on his "yacht"—which turned out to be not the large sort of pleasure craft Kelly normally associated with the term, but rather an overly cramped sailboat designed not for comfort but for speed, Johannsen explained.

"She's a racer!" he shouted, the freezing early-morning wind drowning out his voice even before they began moving. "She cost a fortune, but wait till you see her speed!"

Johannsen picked Kelly up at her hotel at five-thirty with plans for an early start. She had forced herself to get up at five and, thankfully, force down a donut and coffee.

Within ten minutes on the water, though, Kelly found herself on the verge of being seasick, as much from the light waves in the bay as from having to constantly duck and switch positions every time Johannsen wanted to move the sail, which was pretty much all the time.

In fact, he did not appear to be a particularly experienced sailor, either, as he kept moving the sail to one side, stopping and cussing, then moving it to another, only to stop and cuss again—and each time forcing Kelly to duck and reposition herself elsewhere on the cold, hard, seatless deck.

"You'll get used to it! Just got to get your sailor's footing," Joahnnsen shouted in between curses.

"Great boat!" Kelly lied, remembering how she had once gotten seasick on a floating pool lounge.

"Got an engine that runs on biodiesel! When I need it. 'Course, she runs greenest and cleanest on the wind!"

But for Kelly it was wind that was cold, very cold. And worse, in addition to being iced by the wind, every few moves of the sail would hang one side of the boat so low that water splashed up and hit both of them.

"Got to get you a sailing jacket like this one. They cost an arm and a leg, but they break the wind almost completely—and they're waterproof!"

"Wow! Great!" Kelly affirmed as a spray of water hit her cold in the face. Kelly longed for the old days, when a man would not brag about how warm *his* coat was but rather would offer it to her so *she* would be warm. So much for woman's liberation, Kelly thought, shivering.

Three hours later they were seated at a trendy café whose interior design promised more of the Golden State's gourmet food, which Kelly had been suffering all these weeks.

Johannsen looked dry and together. His clothes appeared freshly pressed, his hair neatly combed.

Kelly, conversely, looked as if a cat had just dragged her in out of a typhoon, and then dragged her back out again not liking what it saw. Her normally smooth, straight hair seemed now to stand on end in spots, her clothes were wet and wrinkled, and her face had a frightful look of horror embossed on it.

Kelly had only barely fought off being sick on the boat, a great way to impress a boss who was offering her a promotion, and all knowing a turning point in her career was on the line: Look good on George Johannsen's "yacht" and the world could be hers; vomit on it and it wasn't entirely certain she wouldn't have to *swim* back to shore.

Kelly looked at the menu.

Seven-grain waffles with blueberry compote. Tofu sausage—but don't worry; it's flavored with low-fat maple syrup. "Fiber-filled" wheat and oat porridge. High-protein fruit smoothies "ideal for the digestion . . ."

Kelly was fairly sure that putting the word *digestion* on a menu was illegal in the state of New York.

And once again her emotions swung back to wishing she *had* vomited on Johannsen's yacht, so she would not be promoted, so she would not be made to stay in this infernal land any longer. She continued down the menu and decided that drowning at sea might in fact have been a better fate than being served an eggplant and broccoli omelette, crusted and topped with low-fat Oriental salad dressing.

Unsure whether she could stomach such delicacies, Kelly told

Johannsen she had eaten a protein bar before leaving the hotel—people in California seemed to be crazed about protein bars—and was watching her calorie intake, and with this excuse she got away with ordering just coffee.

Which turned out to be a whole added ordeal in itself, since the "café" served "a wide array of the finest gourmet coffees," but a customer new to the menu would need an orientation course (and probably be asked to take an exam) to even begin to understand it.

Kelly finally managed to order something called Sumatra mocha-something cappuccino al la something with a dash of something else, and she ordered the "Captain's" size because it was in the leftmost column (on a menu with no prices), a position she wrongly assumed would list the smallest size—and thus the least she would have to digest in her current, still-seasick condition . . .

Which turned out to be the largest, and, worse, it was ice coffee with all kinds of sweet stuff added—enough sugar in a single cup, Kelly calculated, to offset a week of whole-grain pancake and tofu sausage dieting.

Making matters worse, the room was still rocking, and rubbing salt into her seasickness, Johannsen ordered a giant breakfast that towered over the plate, forcing Kelly to see and smell first-hand the specter of maple tofu bacon and blueberry compote, as she was forced to sit and watch him chomp his way through it all.

Hoping the taste of coffee would overwhelm the olfactory sensation of maple tofu bacon and aged sweet potato hash browns, Kelly sipped at her cup and came to the definite conclusion that the Dutch would have been better off leaving the coffee industry in the sole hands of the Arabs and letting the Sumatrans continue to grow tea, or whatever it was Sumatrans grew back then.

And making matters worse came the issue at hand.

"I'm firing Walker tomorrow afternoon," Johannsen said.

Kelly tried not to choke on her coffee.

"I've arranged to bring the entire board out with us. We'll see what Walker has to say about this hang glider nonsense, and he'll be left looking as crazy as he is and without a leg to stand on."

"Somehow I don't know if it'll go that smoothly," Kelly said. "There's something about Bernard . . ."

Johannsen's demeanor changed. He squared his face and gave Kelly a serious scowl.

"I brought you out this morning, Kelly, to get to know you on a deeper level. I have to know that you're going to back me up and back our company up. You're the person I've hand-picked to become the new CEO, and I have to know that you're on board one hundred percent."

"I am *quite* on board, George," she said, feeling the room sway as if she were still on board the boat. "You know I am."

"Good. We're going to need to take swift action to find out where things are on 'Murder Mystery 2' and other titles in the pipeline, and how to contain whatever mess and whatever waste Walker has left us."

"Right . . ."

"What, you look doubtful."

"It's just . . . it's just . . . I don't know. It seems like everything is a game to Bernard, and I get the feeling he doesn't often lose games."

Chief O'Brian had never been in a video game shop before and might as well have just walked into an astrophysics library for all that he was able to comprehend around him.

He waited patiently at the counter for more than five minutes while several children in front of him argued over which game to buy with the twelve dollars they had between them. He finally got the attention of the clerk, who wasn't a lot older than the kids arguing over games.

"I'm looking for a video game," O'Brian said. It sounded like a plea for salvation, and in fact made for a pretty silly announcement given that he was in a shop that sold nothing but video games.

"You came to the right place," the teenage clerk said cheerfully. "PlayStation games are on this wall, Wii games are over by the door, along with Wii accessories, Xbox games are on the right, and PSP and Game Boy games are here next to the counter. Or are you looking for Nintendo DS? Or the old Nintendo GameCube?"

O'Brian turned paler. "Wha—, wha—, what does all that mean?"

"What game console are you buying a game for?"

"I haven't any idea!" O'Brian said shaking his head in disbelief. "I'm looking for a game called 'Murder Mystery.' It's made by a company called OffCide Studios."

"Ah, well, that title is available for several consoles."

"Which does it work best on?" O'Brian asked, not really understanding.

"I like it best on Wii, though your arms get a little tired."

"How much would that run me?"

"The game is thirty-nine ninety-nine."

"For a video game?!"

"Yeah. If you want to buy a Wii, we have a pretty good bundle for one-fifty."

"You can still buy something for a dollar fifty?" O'Brian asked.

"No, dude, a hundred and fifty dollars."

"A hundred and fifty dollars?!" O'Brian looked around the store with new respect for these kids, most of them under four feet tall, who had their parents spending hundreds of dollars buying them video games.

And after a hesitation, he took out his police ID and said: "I'll tell you what, I'll buy both the game and the console and I'll pay you another hundred and fifty dollars to go to my house and get it running. This is official police business."

O'Brian added that last statement partially to get the kid to trust him and partially because he fully intended to expense the purchase to the city.

🎮 🎮 🎮

Chen Li strolled past the bus stop, deciding to walk the twenty-five minutes to his dorm rather than fight his way onto one of Beijing's jam-packed buses.

The Monday morning rush-hour pollution was off to a good start for the week, with only a few blocks visible in the distance.

A thirty-minute drive behind him to the east, the street cut between Tien An Men Square and the famous gate of the

Forbidden City, Beijing's most-famous tourist sights. Beyond that a ways was a storm of modern office buildings that housed software workers and others.

That was not the direction in which Chen Li worked or lived.

On the west side of the city was the beat-up old building Chen Li's company had turned into a dormitory for workers from outside Beijing, a building nearly as run down as the office Chen had just left.

His company was not one of those that got modern office blocks and other amenities.

Chen had been working for sixteen hours straight, along with his team. Now he was finally headed home for sleep just as the rest of the city was loading onto buses, bikes, and cars to get to work.

Neither Chen nor his colleagues cared if they got paid for the past day of work. The modeling they were creating was fun and Bernard had promised to give each of them a full copy of the finished product.

Chen certainly didn't want to go back and work for their previous client, the company that made pest control training videos for people in rural parts of the country.

About ten minutes down the road, he came to a small breakfast stand and stopped for a cup of *doujiang,* or fresh soy milk. As he sipped he looked down at his laptop and the new modeling.

Chen was proud of their work. They had gone at it all night and had given Bernard more detail than he had asked for.

Chen would go on to his dorm room, which during the day would be thankfully empty, and navigate through the models one more time, play some of the hang glider scenarios once more— and then send Bernard his results before falling to sleep.

🐦 🐦 🐦

By Sunday afternoon, Bernard's attorney had spoken with the law firm that represented the oceanic institute, and Dr. Sharma was elated at the prospect of a very unexpected grant.

About six o'clock, Bernard pulled her up for an Internet videoconference.

"You understand, sir, I cannot actually *rent* the small research vessel to you." Sharma said. "It is essential to be trained to operate or use one of these."

"Ma'am, I'll have you know I took third place or higher four years in a row in the statewide 'Killer Sub' competition when I was in high school."

"That's a video game?"

"Yes. Considerably archaic graphics by current standards but one of the finest of its time."

"I'll have *you* know there is a considerable difference between a video game submarine and a real research vessel."

"Like what?"

"Well, for one thing, video games don't have to deal with insurance companies. Ours would have me locked up if I let anyone outside the institute touch that sub—even if you *were* trained, which you are not. And for another thing, you would almost certainly find yourself caught on something and probably dying in no time at all."

"No, 'Killer Sub' had several get-lost-and-die scenarios. But come to think of it, insurance companies might make interesting obstacles in several video games I can think of. Hey, there's an idea: a game titled 'Insurance Fraud.' "

"Yes, all the same, we cannot let you in the vessel. But we could operate it for you, if you would be willing."

"That will be good enough. And the sub is connected to a research boat?"

"Correct."

"That means you can send imagery from the sub up to the surface?"

"Instantly, as we see it below. It's all hard-wired—that's one advantage of being connected to a boat on the surface. And from the surface we can send imagery and even video out via mobile network."

"Good. I know it's hard to believe, but you will be searching for an item that will help solve an actual murder."

"Honestly, at this point I think I can believe almost anything." She put on an I-can-believe-anything face. "Now, what is it that you will be looking for, or having us look for, on the ocean floor?"

"A hang glider."

Beyond a raised eyebrow, Sharma lost all expression, along with the I-can-believe-anything face.

🐦 🐦 🐦

Sunday evening. Bernard and Lester sat talking side by side, except that each was next to the other in a laptop videoconference, Bernard in his Cliff Shores studio and Les at his townhouse in Daly City, just outside of San Francisco.

"Chen Li managed to come up with some fast modeling," Lester said. "So I take it Johannsen wasn't intimidating enough?"

"Let's just say that the thought of going back to producing 3-D virtual training animation for home pest control in the countryside was enough that Chen Li was willing to work for free," Bernard responded with a less-than-innocent smile.

Before each of them, though separately, were two large-screen TVs displaying modeling that they were able to navigate around in with avatars, either on foot or by hang glider. Bernard's avatar had a striking resemblance to Sean Connery, though still the shape of Bernard—kind of like what James Bond would look like if he had spent his entire life sitting around, eating, and playing video games instead of saving the world, drinking martinis, and charming gorgeous women.

"Fantastic work they did, though, you have to admit," Lester said. "Look, they even put in those funny-looking birds up by the cliffs."

"You're the one who said we have to have a complete world to solve the murder."

Spread about Bernard were three sandwiches, two open bags of potato chips, a pack of chocolate-chip cookies, and a large bottle of Pepsi. Lester, meanwhile, could be seen alternating between licking the white filling from between Oreo cookies and pouring coffee from a fancy espresso machine set next to his laptop.

"But I don't know if I'd want to hang glide in those birds' front yard," Les added. "They're kind of mean looking."

"They look like freaks of evolution to me," Bernard agreed. "I have to believe one of their ancestors was taking a nap when the species suddenly moved on to a more-evolved state."

The modeling's reality was almost scary. Everything looked real, at least until Bernard or Lester would suddenly start walking up the face of a building.

"Hey, this is cool: You even get to choose your hang glider."

"I asked for that. That is the most-essential part," Bernard said. "Each has its own flight capabilities, possible speeds, and ability to stay aloft carrying certain weights. It's no different from an auto racing game where players get to choose their cars based on speed and maneuverability. And color, of course."

"And, wow, color! This one has a motor and I'm going to make it fire red!" Lester exclaimed through an Oreo cookie from the laptop beside Bernard.

Fire red. This was a kid who drove a gray Toyota Prius, Bernard noted.

"They make some weird models with motors," Bernard said. "Eric did the research on that one. Turns out that only a hefty-size hang glider would have the capability of lifting both a rider and the victim, let alone delivering the body to the pigeon coop and setting it down lightly. But, and this is really cool: They make weird, weird hang gliders with motors," Bernard added with his eerie game smile.

"I have to try this one out," Lester said

"Chen Li said in his email that he managed to get the body near the coop from a spot on the hill," Bernard said. "It was from there, where that red bookmark tag is. But he said he had a hard time keeping the body high enough to get it on the coop."

Bernard took a bite from a pastrami and cheese sandwich and used his avatar to scout about the hill behind his house.

"What about that ritzy apartment building? Could a hang glider take off from the roof of that?" Bernard asked.

"It would have to be one crazy son of a bitch. Though to be honest, the willingness to jump off cliffs indicates a certain lack of touch with reality to begin with, if you ask me. I imagine there would be heavy winds up on that building."

"Let's go see what Chen Li and his friends put up there. He had images from our aerial shoot."

Bernard and then Lester suddenly began walking up the outside of the eight-story building, zigzagging around balconies along the way.

When they got to the top they found themselves in a sort of rooftop garden.

Much of the north side of the roof was built over with tall thick-glass windows looking out toward North Cliff; the south was open and furnished with a row of tables down the center, and plants and garden statues. All of this was surrounded by a four-foot-high wall, making it safe to walk to the edge.

Bernard pushed a key on his keyboard, and sure enough, just as he had expected, a pop-up advisory appeared, giving him a temperature and wind measurement.

Bernard pushed another key and a menu came up allowing him to choose a hang glider. He selected a motorized model. Lester did the same.

Another menu let them attach the victim's body, and they got to choose how long of a rope it would hang by, where and how the rope would be attached, and importantly, whether the victim was still alive and conscious—and likely flapping around if he were, given the prospect that he was about to be impaled on a pigeon coop.

And another pop-up menu showed how to get started. Bernard and Lester then took to jumping off the roof, but in every case failing to make the body clear the wall, and as a result causing their avatars to bounce down the side of the building and bash onto on the ground, where they would be met by the opening notes of "Taps": Duh, duh-duh . . . duh, duh-duh . . .

"I don't know anything about hang gliding," Bernard said, "but from what I've seen, they often have a good stretch or ramp from which to start, and they're already getting a lift before they . . . find themselves with a sudden lack of ground beneath them."

"There's no way to do that here, not with the wall around the roof."

Bernard looked around again. "Hey, the tables. Why are they all lined up in a row like that?"

Lester quickly jumped his avatar up onto the row of six tables, which cut the open area in half from the back side and pointed toward the water.

He hit a key that made his avatar run. And sure enough, by the time he got to the end of the tables, he had substantial lift.

He pushed a key for more and got it—but only to have the body hit the safety wall, stretch the rope, and slap Lester down into the side of the building.

When Bernard finished laughing, he looked over at Lester on the laptop and said, "Hey, let me try something."

He pulled up the victim menu and selected a longer rope length.

"Let's assume that anybody who is considering hang gliding with a body from the top of a high-rise building is, well, as we said, a few french fries short of a Happy Meal," Bernard said. "But let's also assume he is a pretty good hang glider. Now watch this."

Bernard ran down the row of tables as Lester had and got lift as well, but the extra slack in the rope allowed him turn and lift higher, then higher, above the roof. And from there he was able to slowly lift the body up.

As he swooped in a circle above the roof, the body gradually followed him higher and higher until it was above the wall level. Bernard then turned the hang glider toward the water and took to flight.

Lester pulled up a preview menu and put himself in the air watching everything from above, as the hang glider and body flew straight at the pigeon coop.

Bernard paused the game and looked at Lester.

🎮 🎮 🎮

Kelly Chambers returned to her hotel room Sunday evening with two full grocery bags.

Her legs were weak and the added shakiness nearly made her sick. This was one day she needed to get over.

She was still in a state of motion sickness from the "yacht" ride earlier, a condition aggravated considerably by watching Johannsen eat piles of "gourmet" healthy breakfast food, while she pretended to enjoy coffee that sat in her stomach like lice. Sweetened and gourmet lice, but lice.

And Johannsen couldn't leave it at that. After the meal he insisted on driving Kelly to his mansion to meet the family.

He lived in a huge house, two stories high with three-story-high ceilings in the central area—a grandiose mansion that Kelly quickly decided was the ugliest house she had ever laid eyes on. It had a pretentious grand architecture that attempted to mix Greek columns with Mexican adobe walls, and it was filled everywhere with different types of art work that failed utterly to blend together.

Johannsen insisted on walking Kelly through the entire circus, all twenty or more rooms, and explain the significance and story behind each piece of art.

That was followed by an agonizing tea session with Johannsen's wife, who talked incessantly about the charity work she did ("I decided I wanted to strive for great achievements even though we're already rich and don't need to . . .") and Kelly was then made to sit through a thirty-minute piano recital by Johannsen's "prodigy" eight-year-old son, who failed to get all the notes of "Twinkle Twinkle Little Star" correct.

And finally, just to add a last bit of discomfort to the day, Johannsen drove her back to her hotel in the little electric death trap he called a car.

And now, the day finally over, Kelly was back at the hotel, safe from any further torture from Johannsen and Northern California.

She reached into one of the bags and pulled out a fifth of Johnny Walker Black Label, which she quickly opened and methodically made a drink with—two shots of scotch, two ice cubes, and a splash of water.

This she downed in one long draw, then made another, and with that in her hand, she sat down and turned on both the TV and her laptop, hoping noise or other stimuli would make her forget the water, the cold, the boat, the breakfast, the art, the wife, the son . . .

An hour later Kelly had finished two minimart hot dogs, a minimart hamburger, and the better part of a bottle of white wine. French wine. Kelly had grown so tired of listening to Johannsen brag about the wondrous wine country north of San Francisco— and then not letting her drink any—that she took special pleasure in buying French wine, which, curiously, was less expensive than its Northern California counterparts.

And once fed, she climbed into a hot bath, which, proving one version of Murphy's Law, caused the phone to ring—or, rather, her laptop.

She got out of the bath, slipped a towel around her, and walked out to look.

It was Johannsen calling for a videoconference.

Ignoring the call she picked up a magazine and returned to her bath.

🦟 🦟 🦟

Bernard and Lester, virtually on the same rooftop but an hour's drive apart in brick-and-mortar terms, began to inspect their surroundings.

"I think we definitely have something here," Lester said.

"I would say we do," Bernard agreed. "We may be on the verge of answering several questions—including *who* the victim was and what the motive was."

"Hopefully who the murderer is, too."

The detail Chen Li and his team had produced of the rooftop was phenomenal, all based on aerial photographs.

In the covered section, Bernard and Lester could see two telescopes aimed out at the ocean and at the cliff. A shelf on one side also held two pairs of binoculars.

On a table in the outside section, another pair of binoculars sat along with several books and a drink. Unfortunately the detail did not include titles or pictures on the book covers.

"What would the police do at this point?" Lester asked.

"Forget the police," Bernard said. "What would Sherlock Holmes do?"

"Sherlock Holmes in the old BBC version or Sherlock Holmes played by Robert Downey Jr.?"

"Sherlock Holmes in general," Bernard said.

"Sorry, pick one. My imagination doesn't work unless I have an image in mind."

"Oh, OK . . . make it Adrian Monk. What would Adrian Monk do?" Bernard asked.

"Adrian Monk would look at details—details no one else could see."

"Unfortunately, as good of work as Chen Li did, we cannot see beyond the detail he saw and thought to add to the modeling."

Bernard and Lester looked at each other briefly, then both separately turned to laptops and began searching.

Bernard lit up an additional large-screen TV and began looking through thousands of thumbnails—mini samples of the tens of thousands of images they had collected around Cliff Shores, including rather expensive aerial imagery that Bernard was sure to get into trouble for.

These were the images behind the modeling.

After a few minutes Lester looked back. "Found the building," he said. "I'll pass you the link." He passed the link to the images' server location to Bernard, who quickly opened the folder on the TV screen.

A moment later both were studying substantially more detail of the rooftop, as it had been shot from the air.

"Zoom up around the telescopes," Lester said. "There are a bunch of books and spiral notebooks."

"I just popped an image of the books on the table into Photoshop," Bernard shot back. "By changing the color levels, I can just make out the titles. They appear to be bird-watching books."

"Well, that makes sense, seeing the binoculars and telescopes. I can just see detail on one book inside. It appears to have a bird on the cover."

Bernard glanced at Lester, then lit another TV screen with video he had shot of the hang gliders at North Cliff the previous afternoon—and the funny-looking birds flying out at them.

"Hhhmmm . . ." Bernard sighed.

15

Monday morning.

Early Monday morning Bernard knocked on Limei's door, the first time he had dared approach the house while her grandparents were home. The grandmother answered, and Bernard, with a look of terror on his face, asked for Limei, who thankfully appeared from behind.

He handed her a key to his studio and a piece of paper with instructions, then high-stepped it to his car and drove off.

Limei opened the paper and saw a diagram of tables and TV screens.

It appeared she had some work to do.

Four-thirty, Monday morning.

George Johannsen awoke at the same ungodly hour he did each morning and went for his regular five-mile run before sitting down to a granola and fruit breakfast, served with soy milk and ginseng tea.

While eating he scanned the Wall Street Journal, the New York Times, and several other publications on his iPad, then checked his email.

Everything was on schedule. A fleet of limos would carry the entire five-member board of directors down to Cliff Shores, where Walker would be disposed of once and for all.

Monday morning, a more-reasonable though less-than-pleasant hour.

Chief O'Brian eyed his morning coffee through a haze. Sitting in the kitchen wearing a bathrobe, he felt nauseated, and his arms hurt so badly he could barely lift them to get at the badly needed caffeine.

The teenage clerk from the video game store had come to O'Brian's house to hook up the Wii game console and show him how to play "Murder Mystery." O'Brian could barely make sense of how it worked.

It appeared to be a combination of police action and a forensic investigation as various characters—one or more of them the bad guys—went around trying to solve a murder. Along the way they were met by thugs trying to scare them off the case, as well as deadly booby traps set by murderers and conspirators.

O'Brian watched the boy play it for ten minutes, then fooled with it himself for ten, and finally concluded the purchase had been a mistake and that anyone who could play such a game, let alone start the company that designed it, was simply stupid.

But before the clerk left, he inserted a disk that had come with the Wii console bundle, and a menu lit up showing Wii sports: bowling, golf, baseball, boxing, and more. Within minutes O'Brian was hooked and, his wife still in Hawaii, he wound up spending much of the night swinging baseball bats and golf clubs and tennis rackets, and boxing with computer opponents.

The lightweight remote attachments, along with the kindness of the games, made him feel forty years younger.

But one thing the store clerk had failed to tell O'Brian about was that the first few times you play a Wii sports game, you should not play too long—just as you should not go and bowl five lines at first try or play thirty-six holes of golf on your first round.

O'Brian felt severe pain in muscles he didn't know existed, from the top of his shoulders and neck to the tips of his fingers.

O'Brian had bought the console and game so that he could waltz into the afternoon's meeting ready and well-informed. Now, brooding at the distance of his coffee and wearing only a bathrobe, he wondered seriously how he was going to put his clothes on with his arms out of action.

Monday morning, unpleasantly early due to an impatient sunrise.

Captain Toland opened his eyes to a shooting pain in his back. He had slept off and on during the night—more off, less on—in the front seat of his squad car, parked just down the alley from Bernard's studio.

It irked Toland to no end that he had been posted to sleeping in his car in order to be on hand *if Walker needed him*. Toland felt his mission ought to be arresting someone, possibly even Walker himself—not sleeping in a car in an alley to assist some fruitcake who was playing video games, now at county expense.

Toland reached down to the passenger-side floor and produced a red Thermos and a metal coffee cup.

He needed desperately a hot cup of coffee, and after filling the cup, he almost smiled as it neared his mouth—only to discover the coffee had long since gone cold. It seemed that he had been drinking a lot of cold coffee as of late.

Suddenly he noticed Walker's car was moving, and before he could react, Bernard whipped by.

Toland searched franticly for the keys, which he never left in the ignition if he knew he might fall asleep. Finding them under a newspaper, he slammed the car into gear and sped down the alley to where Bernard had turned—and promptly found no sign of him.

But he did catch sight of the Thermos spilling across his lap and much of the front seat as he screeched to a halt.

Cursing, he raced up the side road to the highway above—and again found no sign of Walker.

"Shit," he said, knowing he was about to get in trouble for losing his charge, and possibly show up at the meeting looking as if he had wet his pants.

Monday morning, not so early.

Lester Argyle awoke after only a few hours of sleep; he and Bernard had been up nearly all night running through the simulations.

Argyle sped through his elaborate morning coffee ritual as he had to get quickly on the road and pick up the other engineers, and make sure he got them to Cliff Shores on time.

He brought a portion of greasy dark Mandheling coffee beans to a medium grind and loaded the coffee filter, then washed the pot thoroughly and filled it with ice-cold water from the refrigerator filter. In moments the thick aroma of coffee filled the air.

Les had been dreaming for the past two hours that he was hang gliding, something about hang gliding and a murderer . . . and only the smell of coffee reminded him of the simulations, of the images behind his dreams.

Les had read how smells reacted with memory, how whole emotional states could be recalled by a sudden scent. He had been working so long on this murder business without result that the smell of coffee, which Les drank all the time, was beginning to depress him.

But with the progress of the weekend, suddenly it again smelled sweet as gold.

Monday morning, painfully early.

The morning wake-up call greeted Kelly Chambers with a full-blown hangover.

She rolled over in bed moaning, reckoning she hadn't been hungover since college, and at least then she had had fun earning it.

Looking at the clock she realized she'd overslept ten minutes, but she still called room service and ordered breakfast along with a Bloody Mary, then climbed into a cold shower with hopes of making herself look more presentable.

Forty-five minutes later, she was dressed and fed, her nerves greased by vodka, tomato juice, and Tabasco sauce. Kelly had learned that the only thing she could count on finding when she traveled on business, whether in California or London or Singapore, was a good Bloody Mary.

She lay on the bed again and rested.

At least she had been smart enough to arrange a ride with Lester Argyle, giving Johannsen the excuse that she could better keep an eye on the engineers that way—"a real trouper" she was being, Johannsen said.

In reality Kelly far preferred to ride crammed into a crowded Prius driven by Argyle than in the little electric death trap that Johannsen insisted on zipping about in. And she was also planning to flirt with Les a bit in hopes of getting custody of the front passenger seat.

⁂

Noontime.

Limei glanced around Bernard's studio. It looked completely different now. She had arranged the five large-screen TVs in a U-shape, windows to their back and facing an odd assortment of chairs arranged where the desk had sat.

The desk she had managed somehow on her own to push to the rear of the room.

She leaned down, pushed a key, and woke up the one laptop where she knew Bernard had some of the modeling.

A menu popped up with the option to play a preview. She clicked on Play and a TV screen lit up, showing a hang glider with a body hanging from a rope.

It had occurred to Limei that Bernard might just be off his rocker with this hang gliding business, as her grandparents had insisted he was. Now she knew different.

Now she *knew for certain* he was a screwball. And he would be of no help to her grandfather.

⁂

Noontime.

As hard as she tried not to, Kelly still got stuck in the backseat of the Prius, crammed between Tom Dirks and Eric Lyle, both loaded with devices.

The tight quarters reminded her suddenly that she was claustrophobic. And the movement as Lester darted around in the little car did not make her feel any better.

It quickly got worse. As they pulled onto Highway 101, Tom, Eric and an engineer Kelly didn't know in the front passenger seat all pulled out laptops and began passing wires about to connect them. Apparently a fourth laptop in the front was being set up as a server and then hardwired to the others so they could go through the modeling along the drive.

All this was done with loud, argumentative discussion that abated only when the screens were live and the game started.

Kelly didn't dare look. On the ride back the previous Saturday, the four of them had played some sort of Internet-based combat game in which they shot at each other, a game that included blood and other gory graphics.

And now with nowhere to turn her head Kelly finally caught a glimpse of what they were playing and her mouth dropped wide open.

All three were flying hang gliders and it didn't take long to notice that the virtual world they were flying in was Cliff Shores.

They soared and rolled and swung around to soar and roll again, all looking down to the sand and water and the alleys along the beach. The sight made Kelly dizzy.

And the cliff. Each time one of them got close to the cliff, he would be attacked by the oddest-looking birds.

And within minutes the noise level picked up again as the three began cheering. Kelly looked closer and saw that something seemed to be hanging from each of the hang gliders. She looked closer, tried to focus better, then realized they had bodies dangling beneath them. No, not all of them. One had a large *live person* flapping his arms and legs about, hanging in the air.

Kelly felt herself getting carsick. Bending forward, she managed to rest her head on one side and focus her attention out the right-side window, hoping the passing landscape might take her mind off flying bodies, and flying live victims more so.

A steady line of cars was passing the slower Prius, which, Lester had explained, achieved even better mileage if you maintained just the right speed.

To Lester Argyle, even the car was a video game.

More vehicles sped forward: a van, a small truck, and then a pair of stretch limousines. Yes, that was how Kelly would be traveling back in New York. She would be cruising in luxury in a stretch limo, not crammed into the back of a Prius. But this, at least, was a far cry better than riding in the rickety electric golf cart with George Johannsen.

Johannsen had actually called again just before Kelly left the hotel and tried to persuade her to ride with *him*. Hah! No way.

She stared out and imagined herself inside of one of the limos. There would be a TV screen playing Bloomberg News, a refrigerator, a wet bar . . . She would be nursing her hangover with a Bloody Mary and would be looking out on the poor suckers around her who were crammed into uncomfortable cars stuck in the morning traffic.

That was why Kelly had gone to grad school at the University of Pennsylvania's Wharton School of Business. So she could ride in luxury.

The windows on the two stretch limos were tinted but Kelly could see into them just well enough to make out that, yes, there was in fact a TV screen in the front one. And, and, and . . . she couldn't quite make out the faces, but no, she wouldn't know the occupants, she was sure.

Moments later, the first limo had moved ahead and the second came squarely into view. Kelly squinted her eyes and made out that it too had a video screen, and that its occupants were sipping beverages. How she longed to be riding in that comfort, and how uncomfortable she felt now, on the verge of throwing up, and stuck among video screens of hang gliders hanging murder victims in Lester's backseat.

Kelly tried to focus on the three occupants of the rear limo, tried to see in, then began to make out the shape of their heads, hair, eyes, noses—and her heart dropped.

One of them was Johannsen and the other two, no doubt, were board members. The front limo, then, was carrying the other board members, with a seat left empty—a seat that had been meant for Kelly.

"Pull over! I'm going to be sick!" Kelly shouted at Lester, who was wearing a four-hundred-and-fifty-dollar headset that was guaranteed to block out all outside sound.

🐦 🐦 🐦

Noontime.

Police Chief O'Brian pulled his unmarked car up behind Captain Toland's patrol car and walked to the driver's side window, where inside Toland sat beside Sergeant Bill Peterson in the passenger seat.

"It's almost time. We're going to make an arrest today. We're going to go up there and we're going to listen to what this nut has to say, because that's what we've been ordered to do. But when everyone sees he's just a nut, we're going to arrest Wang. That's one character that's been running around loose too long."

Toland took on a resolute look and nodded. As for Peterson, he began bouncing in his seat like a nine-year-old on Christmas morning.

"I'd be willing to make the arrest, sir," Peterson said, an offer met by silence. "I mean, if you need somebody to . . ." His voice trailed off at the sight of grim expressions around him.

O'Brian continued.

"Toland, I want you to be in the room and ready to detain him as soon as I say so. You got that?"

"No problem. My pleasure."

"What should I do, sir?" Peterson asked.

O'Brian frowned and hesitated. Then, "As soon as Walker is done talking, you slip out the door and wait down here by the car—in case someone tries to run for it," O'Brian said conspiratorially, thinking actually it would be better not to have Peterson in the way upstairs.

And with that O'Brian raised an eyebrow toward Toland, indicating Peterson, and stepped back—and, screaming, dove to the ground to avoid being run over by Lester Argyle's silent Prius.

Lester parked and got out with a wide smile.

"This car is silent as a mute eating glue," he shouted to a shaken O'Brian. "Is that cool or what?"

🎮 🎮 🎮

Bernard's studio had become severely uncomfortable. Seated sullenly on one side in office chairs were Johannsen, the board members, and Kelly, whose pale face betrayed her discomfort. Worse, they all kept looking in her direction, as the scantily clad Princess Leia next to her held their attention, and made her all the more uncomfortable at the same time.

Sitting awkwardly and showing it on the other side of the room, in garden chairs, were Mayor Dennings, City Manager Kramer, and Police Chief O'Brian, the latter wearing a scowl that betrayed how little he appreciated being there. Toland and Peterson stood in the rear, while Limei stood outside the door, at the top of the outside stairwell, watching for Bernard.

Bernard was due at one-thirty, and now, at one-fifty, faces were turning red. Mayor Dennings worried about his community center, Kramer thought about O'Brian hiding in Hawaii, O'Brian thought about Toland losing Bernard, who now was the hated focus of Johannsen, whose dark expression set the tone for the other board members, prominent business leaders unaccustomed to being made to wait . . . and then there was Kelly, who was thinking mainly about Bloody Marys.

Limei looked at the unhappy expressions with a terrified one of her own. Below, she saw her grandfather smoking a cigarette and looking up nervously in her direction.

🐔 🐔 🐔

It was nearly two o'clock when Bernard finally arrived and hustled up the outside stairwell. Limei bit her lip and remained silent as he passed. She was certain something bad was about to happen.

As soon as Bernard entered the room, Johannsen was on his feet.

"Walker," he said calmly but sternly, "your days heading our firm are over."

"What?!" Bernard said. "*Your* firm? It's *my* firm, and thank you for assembling the board. It is time everyone sees what we've been doing."

"What you've been doing is misappropriating funds—or perhaps I should say *embezzling!*"

Bernard turned to the mayor. "I will have you know that I have solved the murder, so you can arrange to remove that abominable bird coop."

Johannsen's expression tightened further.

"Do you have the screens linked?" Bernard asked Lester Argyle, who was sitting on the floor connecting wires to a laptop.

"All correct and ready to go," Les responded.

"Good. Let's give everyone a tour of Cliff Shores."

In seconds, the three center screens lit up with a single view extended across them.

Using a mouse on the floor, Lester made a virtual Bernard walk down the virtual alley.

"Welcome to Cliff Shores, virtually as well as actually," Bernard said to the room, leaning down to operate a laptop on a chair next to Les. "And welcome to a murder scene, virtual now as well as real," he added, indicating with a wave the indescribable pigeon coop behind the screens.

A fourth screen flashed a view of Limei's house with a virtual body hanging from the coop.

Bernard spoke to the room with a grand air: "Now remember, our computer modeling is based on thousands of photos and careful measurements.

"As I said Saturday, the body had to be placed on the coop from above—not by an airplane, which would have sent the body too fast, and not by a helicopter, which would have been too noisy.

"But watch this." Now the fifth screen lit to show video of North Cliff shot two days earlier, with several hang gliders soaring gracefully along the rocks.

"There, look at that one," Bernard said pointing. "This guy looks as if he's not moving at all, and in fact he barely is. And a hang glider is silent, completely silent, so that no one can hear it even if he whips through the sky at a high speed.

"Our initial modeling showed that a typical hang glider would likely fail to lift so heavy a body, as well as the rider, or murderer.

"But a little research found that they do, in fact, make *motorized* hang gliders. Some pretty strange-looking machines, too, as you can see."

Now the fifth screen showed several bizarre-looking hang gliders with various engines and attached vehicles.

"Hhhmmmpth!" O'Brian said. "Wait just a minute. I've got you there. If it had a motor, you would have heard it. It would have woken you up, just like a helicopter would have."

Lester Argyle got that wide smile on his face again. "Just like my Prius?" he asked, and O'Brian fell silent again with a scowl as expressive as Argyle's grin.

🐘 🐘 🐘

Liu Shizheng went into the Beijing office before anyone else arrived, with the aim of seeing what Chen Li and his team had been working on over the weekend.

The jobs from OffCide Studios paid well, and the company's apparent satisfaction with the work made him look good.

But he also had the growing feeling that he was losing control over his workers, who seemed too eager and would often move on on projects without getting his OK first.

It wasn't like that back when they were doing the pesticide animation. In fact, the workers wouldn't do anything without being told to, an attitude that Liu viewed as less than efficient but easily controllable.

And when projects were finished, he looked good, since they were finished only by virtue of his constant nagging.

Now the staff was coming in on weekends and sending finished work off to San Francisco before he even got to see it.

As they had done apparently over the weekend.

Liu sat at Chen Li's computer and turned it on.

It took him only a few seconds to find the new modeling, a long slew of files that had a time stamp from the weekend.

He located one of the final files and loaded it.

Now he would see just what it was that Chen Li was up to.

And he became instantly more confused than when he had started. Before him he found motorized hang gliders flying around with live people and dead bodies hanging from them, and fighting with strange-looking birds and creating huge splatterings of blood every time one of the hanging victims crashed.

Liu shut the modeling sequence down after only a minute, then sat back and sighed.

Maybe the crazy things his teachers had told him about the Americans when he was young were true.

*　*　*

"So the next question," Bernard said, "was from where did the hang glider take off?

"You will remember that the victim was found with a shoe missing. A bright yellow shoe. Well, we found it." Bernard switched the screen to a photo of the shoe in the bush where they had found it.

"I believe the shoe was pulled off the victim's foot when he—or his body—hit the pigeon coop. That would have sent it flying in the direction that the hang glider was traveling."

Faces squinted in silence, everyone struggling to understand, for better or worse.

"Now, looking from the shoe near the beach, where my friend Limei over here and I found it, and back toward the pigeon coop, we can see the direction that the hang glider was coming from."

"Bull," O'Brian said.

"Double bull," Johannsen amended.

Producing a Snickers from a vest pocket, Bernard went on, chewing as he spoke.

"And the spot that looked the most obvious was this one." He walked to the center screen and pointed at the single high-rise building in Cliff Shores.

"The roof of this building, which is called Cliffside Condos, is where the hang glider took off, and I think likely where the murder was committed."

Everyone grimaced in disbelief, including Limei from near the outside stairway door. Bernard's explanation was getting wilder and wilder.

Hitting a few keys, Bernard made the building's roof, along with a Bernard avatar that looked surprisingly like Harrison Ford, appear on the fifth screen.

"With the aid of some rather expensive aerial photography," Bernard said, ignoring Johannsen's now even more contorted expression, "we were able to re-create the rooftop in striking detail. Please pay special attention to the telescopes, the binoculars and especially the manner in which the tables are lined up.

"I am choosing a hang glider with a motor and attaching the victim's body with a rope. Now watch what happens if I try to jump from the side of the building."

In a first try, Bernard's avatar runs and gets just enough lift to slam the body into the safety wall, which tightens the rope and snaps the avatar into the side of the building below, where it is left hanging by the rope.

"Nobody would be stupid enough to try something like that," Chief O'Brian said.

"You are correct. Especially a good hang glider, and I am assuming that anyone who would try to move a body in this way would have to be a particularly good hang glider to begin with. And a good hang glider would not try that. A good hang glider would want a ramp. That's why these tables were arranged in a line. Now observe."

Everyone watched closely—the way onlookers might watch someone have a nervous breakdown—as Bernard's avatar jumped onto the rear of the tables, ran their length, lifted into the air, and rolled and circled until it had enough height to slowly clear the body over the safety wall.

And from there it lost altitude but traveled slowly, straight toward the water, with the body aimed directly at the coop.

"A perfect ride, and the only ride possible, I believe, given the weight," Bernard said.

"You don't think someone would see that flying through the sky?" O'Brian challenged.

"Ah, there is one important piece of data missing from these simulations, and that is the weather data." Bernard pushed a button. "This is what the night really looked like."

Suddenly all that could be seen were blurry lights showing where Bernard's and Limei's houses were.

"We had a marine layer move in that night, according to weather bureau data. Lights would have shown where the buildings were, but it is entirely possible the murderer would not have seen the pigeon coop until it was too late. And it's possible also that the murderer had memorized the route in advance, but had done so *before* the pigeon coop suddenly sprang into existence exactly one week earlier."

"Wow!" Bill Peterson blurted out in excitement, but immediately fell silent when he saw the angry look on O'Brian's face.

🐦 🐦 🐦

Down the alley, along the hill leading up toward the minmart, the bushes shook.

Peering out from between two hedges a pair of eyes stared at the cars along the alley, and looked up to the upper floor of Bernard's house.

A hand rubbed the barrel of a rifle, as if petting a cat.

From the particular vantage point, the heads of several people in Bernard's studio could just be made out—dim targets in the distance.

🐦 🐦 🐦

Bernard looked around the room "Now, watch what happens when I continue the route."

Everyone watched the screen as the hang glider sailed perfectly by the top of Bernard's house, slowing just a slight bit to add lift— then *rip*, the body caught on the coop, the rope came loose, pulling the shoe with it, and the hang glider went crashing toward the water beyond.

"How very convenient!" O'Brian said, standing up. "Your only possible evidence has washed out with the tide. I've had enough of this."

"Don't be so sure," Bernard said loudly, with his commanding, or rather *de*manding, manner.

He clicked another icon and the fourth screen changed to show live video of the inside of the small research sub.

"Can you hear me, Dr. Sharma?"

"Yes, I'm here. Can you hear me clearly?" she replied with her educated accent.

The doubting faces turned their attention to the screen.

"I hear you quite clearly. Everyone, this is Dr. Sharma of the Cliff Shores Institute for Oceanic Research. Doctor, can you tell us where you are and introduce your surroundings a little?"

"Certainly, Mr. Walker. I am currently about one hundred meters offshore directly in front of where the murder victim was found. You were very insistent that this is where I should be for this call.

"Now, much of the coastline in this region has a swift dropoff, or a series of steep canyons, a short distance offshore. The dropoff is particularly close near Cliff Shores, which is one reason our institute located here. And as you can see on this screen, the dropoff is already beginning where I am now."

Bernard cut in. "I am going to blow up your video screen on another monitor here, doctor, so that everyone can see more clearly." With a click the video screen inside the sub appeared on the rightmost TV, showing the marine world around the sub.

"So what did you find in the area, Dr. Sharma?"

Bernard hadn't heard from Sharma yet and was hoping she had found something. Otherwise the best he was going to be able to offer—after only two days—was plans for a wider search, should the hang glider have been washed farther out. But he held his confidence. He had been in tighter spots than this, at least virtual ones, and kept his cool. He took a bite off the Snicker's bar in his hand.

"Did you spot a hang glider in the area, doctor?"

"I'm afraid there is nothing of the sort where you estimated it would be, Mr. Walker."

Bernard choked on caramel. O'Brian took on a satisfied, knowing expression and smiled at Bernard. Johannsen made a similar expression, while Kelly frowned sickly and Limei's eyes teared up.

"You are sure there is nothing in the area, doctor?" Bernard pleaded.

"I am quite certain."

"Show's over, Walker," O'Brian said.

"A lot more than that is over," Johannsen added.

Then Sharma's voice again: "But my assistant here, Dr. Lin, pointed out to me yesterday that even weighed down by a motor, a hang glider could get moved around substantially by the tide. So we went out earlier this morning and did a sonar scan beyond the dropoff. Here is video footage of what we found in the end."

All heads darted back to the right-hand screen, which showed a shiny object in the distance. As the sub approached and the camera zoomed in, more and more of the object's features became visible, and in seconds it became clear that what they were looking at was a very strange-looking, but all the same a very identifiable, hang glider. A hang glider with a long line in the sand that appeared to be . . . yes, a long piece of rope attached to it.

Limei, the engineers, and even the board members suddenly burst out in a cheer, as if at the exciting climax of a movie in a cinema.

O'Brian's and Johannsen's faces went blank. Kelly for the first time that day felt good—though she managed to hide her grin from Johannsen.

And Limei's face took on a new level of disbelief, but one with a smile to it.

🐾 🐾 🐾

Damian's butt hurt, his back was stiff, and his neck surged with pain.

He had been crawling from spot to spot along the hillside for more than two hours, sitting on pointed rocks and straining to look through binoculars from different angles—all while struggling not to be seen from the alley below.

There had to be some way of finding out what was going on in the meeting.

Damian had a rifle with him and he figured at this distance he might be able to take out two or three of the figures visible in the upstairs windows, but he couldn't be sure to get the weird guy. It was the weird guy he needed to get; he knew that now, now that this meeting was at the weird guy's house.

Oh, Damian had been keeping an eye on events the whole time. He had been watching contentedly as the police utterly failed to do anything about the murder, he had been watching time run by, knowing that city officials were going to get more and more comfortable with the notion that a murderer might never be found . . . he had been silently stalking and watching the whole time.

But then the weird guy got involved.

And now Damian thought he could make out the weird guy near the screens, often stepping out of sight behind one. It was easy to guess who many of the other attendees were by the cars parked in front.

The police chief was there; everyone in Cliff Shores knew his car, since it was the only unmarked police car in the city, and though unmarked, it still looked as little unlike a police vehicle as a riot truck might. And that Cliff Shores patrolman was there, too; that police car was regularly seen around Cliff Shores, in donut shops and fast-food restaurants, and at the Beachfront Café. And that county officer who was investigating the murder, he was there; his car had been parked conspicuously around Cliff Shores a lot recently, often with him asleep at the wheel—literally.

With his binoculars Damian had been able to identify the mayor and the city manager as they walked in. He had seen them on TV, on the local-access channel the cable company gave the city. It showed occasional council meetings and other public events, and Damian, with his regular interest in municipal affairs in Cliff Shores, often stayed up late into the night, thinking dark thoughts and exploring the farthest reaches of the cable TV offerings.

And there were also more weird people at the meeting. Five of them had somehow crammed into one of those hybrid cars that always got into Damian's way on the interstate. Japanese hybrid cars were the scum of the earth.

In fact, taking a few potshots at the Prius and the stretch limousines seemed mighty tempting to Damian at the moment.

But fire any shots and the neighborhood would be filled with cops, and Damian didn't need that.

The weird guy had to be killed; that was the priority. Damian had seen him searching the beach, taking pictures, asking people questions, and that morning, that very morning, the weird guy had gone into the Cliffside Condos. Damian saw it from the hillside.

He wouldn't be hard to kill. He lived all alone—Damian had been watching—and aside from these meetings the only person he usually had inside with him was that little girl from across the street. And Damian dreamed about the chance to kill her, to kill anyone that lived in that *damned house across the street*—preferably kill them slowly and painfully . . . that damned house across the street.

That house where some genius had suddenly built that goddamned structure on the roof. Where the hell did it come from? It hadn't been there when he had planned and practiced the route. Why did it have to suddenly pop up on that particular night? My God!

Yes, killing anyone who lived in *that* house would be a pleasure, a memory Damian would cherish forever.

Damian moved to another bush, trying for a better view.

And that was just the spot he needed. It finally afforded an angle that showed one of the video screens.

Damian took out a collapsible but powerful telescope he had stolen from the bird guy's rooftop, trained it on the studio windows, squinted . . . and began to make out the detail . . . and slowly bits and pieces of the screen came into focus. It was . . . it was . . .

It looked like a hang glider. It looked like a motorized hang glider, maybe *the* hang glider.

And just as that sight sunk in, a cheer erupted from inside the house, startling Damian and causing him to slip and slide down the hill about six feet, scraping his arm and throwing his back out along the way.

Six feet lower in elevation with an equal decrease in pride, Damian looked over toward Bernard's with a glare nearly deadly on its own.

The weird guy would have to die very soon, he thought to himself.

16

"I don't goddamned believe it!" O'Brian said, walking over to the screen. "Show me the hang glider going off the building again."

Bernard moved his laptop next to the left-hand screen and pointed.

"Here, have yourself a ball. Use the space bar to start and stop the sequence and the plus and minus keys to zoom in and out."

With a grunt, O'Brian began to run through the hang glider simulation.

"Wait a minute!" Toland interjected. "This is all crazy. So there's a hang glider in the water out there. Cliff Shores has hang gliders out every weekend and sometimes weekdays. There's bound to be one going into the water every now and then. You're just stretching this thing further and further."

"It *is* a rather wild theory," O'Brian agreed. "And you still haven't answered basic questions like (A) who the victim was, (B) who killed him, and (C), *why?*"

Bernard opened an Almond Joy, took a bite, and with his mouth full began to explain.

"Ah, but I have. Look again at the detail on the roof." With a few mouse clicks Bernard lit the three main screens up with the rooftop alone stretched across them. And turning the modeling he offered views of the surroundings.

"You will notice several items: telescopes, binoculars, books . . . and note that while we can't read the titles of the books, we can see photos on this one . . . and this one, and in both cases they appear to be photos of birds.

"What we have here is, the evidence suggests, the home of an ornithologist, a bird expert, or at least an avid bird watcher."

"Because images on the book *look* like birds?" Toland asked. "You're stretching things again here, don't you think?"

"Except that I got close-up photos a little over an hour ago."

Everyone paid attention as Bernard took out his iPhone, pressed a few icons, and sent photos of the books taken *on* the roof to one of the screens. And the books were indeed bird-watching guides.

"And what do birds have to do with hang gliders?" Toland demanded.

Bernard lifted a finger into the air and, clicking on a laptop, pulled up the video footage of the hang gliders again. Several times one of them would circle along the hillside to have one of the odd-looking birds swoop out at it.

"A little Internet research over a microwaved burrito at breakfast came up with this: You see, there was an eccentric ornithologist, a bird expert, who was fighting to ban hang gliding at North Cliff—a total and complete ban. His aim was to protect these funny-looking birds that nest along the cliffside.

"His name was Herbert Lowe.

"Lowe was trying to get a ban on hang gliding there through the courts, through the city, through petitions . . ."

"I remember that crackpot," Mayor Dennings said. "He didn't have a case for protecting those birds—they nest for miles along the coast in this area. His *real* concern was that he had bought a condo here. He wanted to study the birds from home using—" The mayor raised an eyebrow at Bernard.

"Using telescopes?" Bernard offered. "From a rooftop condo? Yes. And this is that condo. *This* is *his* penthouse, the home of Herbert Lowe, ornithologist and, it is important to note, writer. And in fact he did get the attention recently of state officials and there was a good chance that North Cliff might be turned into a local bird preserve by next year, which would have forced the hang gliders to glide along somewhere else."

"It's just too far-fetched," Toland insisted.

"More far-fetched than Limei's grandfather carrying a body that size through the little rooftop trapdoor and getting it onto the coop—which our modeling has proved would have been impossible?!" Bernard responded. "No."

"Wait a minute," O'Brian interrupted. "If you've been into that condo today . . . Do you have a positive match between the body and this—what's his name?—Herbert Law?"

"Lowe—L-O-W-E," Bernard corrected with his mouth full. "Herbert Lowe. And to answer your question, look at this." From his iPhone Bernard produced another image, this one a close-up of one of the books on the outside table. It was titled *Rare Birds of NorCal* and the author listed on the cover was Herbert Lowe.

"So the guy's a writer." Toland challenged. "So what?"

"Well," Bernard said, "let's look at the back cover." From his iPhone he produced another image on the big screen.

From a distance they could see a photo and a promotional blurb.

Bernard zoomed in and the title and photo became clear.

The title read "About the Author" and the photo was, beyond doubt, that of the murder victim.

🐦 🐦 🐦

As soon as he saw the hang glider on the sub video, Sergeant Peterson slipped silently out the door and down to the alley, as he had been instructed.

Peterson didn't realize the plan was just to keep him out of the way—any more than O'Brian had reckoned on there being a need for an officer on the street.

Peterson was intrigued by the wild theory and the screens.

Boy, being caught up in a real murder case, it had not been something Peterson liked at all, until now. Now, with all that was going on, he was beginning to get a whole new perspective on police work. He was beginning to suspect he *was* interested in something more than just solving small-town squabbles.

He strolled down the alley toward the south, reflecting on this new insight.

Unlike Andy Griffith, Sergeant Peterson carried a gun, and he lived, he reflected, in the real world, in a world where people murdered one another and hung bodies on pigeon lofts.

With that thought, he took out his revolver and marveled at it. For the most part the thing scared the bejeebers out of Peterson; it was a pretty dangerous thing to be carrying around, after all.

But now he looked at it with a new adoration.

He continued walking along, eyeing the gun before him, for several more yards, when a movement suddenly caught his attention.

Looking up he saw another set of eyes staring back—a man, a man with a rifle.

The man looked at Peterson, looked at his revolver. Peterson looked at the man, looked at his rifle.

And suddenly the man's foot lost its precarious hold on a rock beneath it and the man fell onto his side and slid several feet down the hill—the movement sending Peterson diving for cover.

When Peterson lifted his head several seconds later, the only trace of the man was the shaking brush through which he had disappeared.

🐔 🐔 🐔

Johannsen stood and walked over to Bernard.

"Great modeling, Walker," he said. "Maybe you can get yourself a job as a police officer. You're going to be looking for something new."

"What?!" Bernard asked, offended at Johannsen's tone.

Johannsen turned to the other board members. "This man has been misappropriating company funds. *All* of this modeling was done with company money. It was embezzlement."

"That is a very serious charge," said one of the board members, a tall Austrian man named Franz Jacobs. "I would hope you could substantiate it."

"Certainly I wouldn't lie about something like this. Oh, and I have screened an interim CEO and possible replacement. She's right here." He indicated Kelly, who turned her head away from Bernard's sudden glare.

"And you have records of Mr. Walker's actions?" Jacobs asked.

"Ms. Chambers here has collected copies of all the relevant documents up to last Friday. Is that not correct, Ms. Chambers?"

Kelly hesitated, a frown on her face. Then weakly, avoiding Bernard's hurt stare: "I'm afraid it is correct."

Joahannsen went on: "And the records show clearly that Walker was ordering *this* modeling from our Beijing outsourcers, and it was all paid for from company accounts?"

Kelly noted now that she was the center of everyone's attention, including that of the girl, who had a tear in her eye.

Kelly looked down, her voice wavered. "Yes, the records are . . . are . . . quite complete."

"That, gentlemen," Johannsen said, "is misappropriation. But more important is this. Ms. Chambers? On the company records, the official company records, what purpose did Mr. Walker state the modeling was for?"

Her eyes on her feet, desperate to avoid Bernard's angry stare, Kelly answered: "It was stated in all the records that the modeling was for video game prototypes."

"Ah-ah! And that, gentlemen, is embezzlement. That is fraud."

The room fell silent, all eyes on Johannsen, Bernard, and Kelly.

Bernard found a bag of Lays Original potato chips in a lower vest pocket, opened it, and began crunching on one loudly as he glared death in Kelly's direction.

"In fact," Johannsen went on, "we have police officers right here in the room, who could do us the service of arresting Walker before he runs off. Arrest him for embezzlement and fraud, is that not correct, Ms. Chambers?"

Kelly looked up sadly at Bernard, then more so at Limei.

And of a sudden, spirit returned to her eyes.

She stood up. "Well, not for fraud or embezzlement, George."

"What do you mean, *Ms. Chambers?*" Johannsen apparently did not like disagreement from his hand-picked replacement.

"The records say the modeling was for research and proto-typing, and to the best of my knowledge, that is correct."

"What?!" Bernard said, the fastest and possibly most-surprised response in the room.

"It's OK, Bernard," Kelly said. "If some of this leaks out now, that won't be all bad."

Johannsen turned a murderous expression on Kelly.

She continued, looking at the board members. "Bernard told me when I first visited him here that the modeling was being used for prototyping for a future Murder Mystery title, and for quality control for 'Murder Mystery 2.' But he said that it had to be kept confidential, even from the board."

"But, but . . ." Johannsen protested. "But we just saw it was for something *completely different!*"

"Well," Kelly replied without emotion, "it was, obviously. But imagine how well *that* is going to sell—a future Murder Mystery title *based on an actual murder*. A bizarre murder, too, I might add."

"What?" Johannsen asked incredulously.

"Is that correct?" Jacobs asked.

"That is correct," Kelly answered, smiling at a perplexed Bernard. Bernard collected himself.

"Yes," he said with uncertainty. "Imagine: a murder mystery video game based on a *real* murder, one that even the police couldn't solve."

O'Brian and Toland shot Bernard a look.

"Uh, no offense," Bernard said, biting from a chip.

"That *is* brilliant," Jacobs said, walking over to get a better look at the glider sequence that O'Brian had been running. "A video game based on an actual murder! Brilliant, yes, brilliant. Absolutely brilliant."

O'Brian walked over to Bernard.

"Walker. I have a good deal of experience working as an officer, as a consultant for police departments, and as a consultant for district attorneys offices, and I have to tell you, this video gaming stuff you're doing right here could be quite lucrative in the law enforcement industry. It might not make it as *evidence* in a court, but it could be used in courts as some very advanced diagramming. And I could see selling it to police departments, district and private attorneys, and a lot more."

Johannsen's eyes opened even wider.

"You don't mean a spinoff, do you?" Jacobs asked.

"Hey, this stuff might be *fun* for teenagers to waste their time on," O'Brian stated, "but it could be of real utility in police investigations. I already have contacts to get started with."

"Well," Jacobs said, "it just so happens that I know a few investors who are looking to focus on police and government agency technology startups. I don't think it would be very difficult to secure seed funding should you decide to create a spinoff business."

Johannsen stared on.

Mayor Dennings walked over. "Well, Walker, a great day it is. We don't yet have the murderer, but we can probably get your view restored now. And of course you'll want to talk about the community center—you do like ballroom dancing, of course, don't you?"

"Wait a minute, wait a minute," Johannsen interrupted. "What about that research sub, Walker? What about that? I suppose you paid for that yourself and did *not* use company funds?"

"No," Bernard said. "Dr. Sharma was kind enough to make the research run for us. Of course, that was *after* I promised to donate funds to help the center buy a new research vessel."

"With company money?!" Johannsen asked.

"No, no. You see, I had set aside a couple million dollars for community relations here in Cliff Shores."

Mayor Dennings raised an eyebrow.

"We had originally envisioned working toward a community center," Bernard said, "but in the interim I was convinced that oceanic research was a far more noble effort to support."

"Wha—, wha—" The mayor couldn't quite form actual words.

Kramer bent his head down to hide a sudden grin.

"Excellent work, Mr. Walker," he said to Bernard, but looking at the floor. Kramer figured he might as well enjoy the situation since he was probably going to be out of a job soon anyway.

"By the way, Chief O'Brian," Kramer added, "I have contacts in city and county offices, police departments, and courts up and down the coast. Let me know if there's anything I can do to help if you do get involved in a spinoff venture like this."

Suddenly Peterson burst in, his gun drawn, his face pale white.

"There's a man with a gun out there!" he said.

Bernard shot back: "There appears to be one in here, as well."

Peterson looked down at his revolver. He'd forgotten he had it out.

O'Brian scowled. "What, you saw a man with a gun and decided someone ought to call a police officer?"

"Uh . . ." Peterson turned red.

Toland took over. "Where did you see him?"

"Just on that side of the building. He was up in the bushes. It looked like he slipped and then ran up the hill somewhere."

Without a word Toland was out the door and headed down. Peterson followed.

"Gentlemen," Chief O'Brian said loudly to the room. "Let's all move away from the windows. Immediately." This got everyone moving, though with uncertainty since the whole upper floor was pretty much all windows.

O'Brian then took out his own revolver and stepped through to the outside stairwell, where he looked down to see Toland and Peterson running around the side of the house.

🐓 🐓 🐓

Going down to the alley himself, O'Brian inspected the area and called for more help. An additional county patrol car and another city car soon arrived.

Toland and Peterson gathered with O'Brian after scouring the hillside.

Toland was at his peak. He loved this sort of excitement. This had finally turned into a real murder case. This was why he had become a police officer.

Still, he was glad the business with Walker was over. The thought of another night in his squad car was horrific.

"It appears clear for the moment," O'Brian said to the two officers.

"He could come back," Peterson said.

"Unless this was some prank or some coincidence, I fully well expect he *will* come back," O'Brian replied. "He was here today—with a gun, whoever he is. He may have been scared away by the police cars."

"Maybe it was the murderer," Peterson offered.

"We have to assume it was," O'Brian said. "Toland, I'm going to ask you to spend another few nights on stakeout here."

"Oh shit," Toland said.

"And Peterson, you're going to sleep in his backseat."

"Oh shit," Toland repeated.

"Yeah, a lot of us are saying 'oh shit' today," O'Brian said.

🎮 🎮 🎮

Fifteen minutes later, much of the group was sipping coffee that Lester Argyle had served—all standing in the back of the room, as far away from the windows as possible—and watching Lester run through various murder scenarios using the Cliff Shores modeling. Operating the screens with a laptop—from a distance—he let the board members try their hand at virtual hang gliding.

Only Mayor Dennings, sitting in a corner near the inside entry, and George Johannsen, sitting next to him, declined to join in the fun.

A short while later O'Brian returned and told everyone it was safe to leave. And it was with a high degree of awkwardness that the group parted.

When all but the engineering team, Limei, and Kelly had left, Kelly finally came face to face with Bernard.

He towered over her like a god trying to decide whether to destroy some lowly being he had accidentally created.

"You were set up to take my job," he said directly.

Kelly hesitated, then, "Ah . . . yeah, sort of."

"Guess 'Murder Mystery 3' ended that, huh?"

"I think it would be safe to say that it did."

"Why? Why'd you suddenly help me?"

"What, are you kidding?" she said, now letting her normally hidden New York accent creep back into her speech. "I couldn't live here. Your Hellfire Jalapeño Hot Dogs are OK, but frankly I could get a better dog from a street vendor in the Bronx. And the pizza here—you guys call that pizza?!"

Bernard looked briefly offended. Then: "The modeling was for a future Murder Mystery title . . ." Bernard repeated Kelly's words. "A pretty slick sudden thought. You not only saved me a lot of trouble, but I believe you have come up with an extremely exciting game plot."

"You think?"

"Well, let's walk up the hill to the minimart—no, apparently there is a man with a gun running around out there. Let's *drive* up the hill and get some lunch. But give me a minute."

Bernard walked over to Limei and led her out the door to the outside stairwell. "I told you I'd solve the murder. Did I lie?"

"No," Limei said, blushing. "I better go tell Grandfather what you did."

🎮 🎮 🎮

Damian sat on the dream balcony of his dream home, licking his wounds with shots of tequila.

He hurt all over.

It was bad enough that he had spent much of the day crawling in the bushes. He had also slipped twice, causing bad scrapes on his arms and on one knee.

Between the pain and worry over the police, Damian didn't even notice the dream view surrounding him. To the left and down the hill slightly was the beach; to the right he looked out on North Cliff, where he could watch hang gliders when he himself was not out. This was why he had bought the house. This is why that stupid bird guy *had to go*.

Well down the beach Damian could make out the weird guy's house, a three-level structure with an outside stairwell, and the house across the street with the *thing* on its roof, the *thing* that had nearly killed him by suddenly coming into being where it hadn't been before. And Damian could see the alley leading up to the buildings, meaning he could watch and see everything that happened.

To the left of that and up the hill a ways he could see that ugly high-class apartment building where the bird guy lived.

And died.

It was those damned birds.

Damian looked out at the cliff, where their nests were visible.

When forcing himself to go to sleep some nights, he would imagine shooting the birds right from his balcony. He could get a high-power rifle with a silencer and have a ball.

But he was saving his bullets for bigger targets—in Bernard's case, a very big one, indeed.

Damian looked down the alley. *That damned rooftop THING. That inexplicable damned thing.*

17

The days that followed seemed to drag on indefinitely for Bernard. He tried to get himself back into planning for "Murder Mystery 2," but couldn't concentrate knowing the murderer was still out there somewhere, and knowing that the man spotted with a gun might be the culprit.

Before this it had never occurred to Bernard that he might be in danger. The murder had just been a nuisance that was keeping him from removing the blasted pigeon coop. But after the gun incident on Monday, Bernard had been scared to go out.

Lester tried to persuade him to stay in the city, but Bernard refused, knowing that Limei and her grandparents were in danger, too, and possibly in worse danger because of him.

So Bernard was not going to run. Instead he went out and spent several hundred dollars on security items, on motion sensors for the ground floor and the outside stairwell, and on extra clamp locks for the windows.

And he knew a police officer was always parked just down the street.

He also made a major food run, buying about two weeks worth of frozen dinners, along with crates of snacks and candy—not to mention three cases of Pepsi.

With this done he spent most of his time at a small desk he set up next to the windows in his studio, where he had a clear view of Limei's house and the alleyway.

Limei stopped over each afternoon to help Bernard scrutinize final modeling for "Murder Mystery 2." But beyond that Bernard saw no one and got little work done.

If the murderer did show up, Bernard would be ready. Unable to concentrate on work, he used his time on preparations for that contingency.

🐻 🐻 🐻

Like Bernard, Damian too spent the next several days looking out from his home. Using his binoculars he could see everything that happened along the alley.

He ate his meals on the balcony, folded laundry on the balcony, used a laptop to read up on the conspiracy by the government and tech companies to control the population of the United States— all on the balcony.

He even moved a small TV out, running a coaxial wire from his cable box, so he could watch the Military Channel and the History Channel, which happened to be running a series each evening on UFO spottings and the related government cover-ups.

And Damian took notes on his balcony, detailed notes about everyone's comings and goings on the alley.

He noted a police car was always parked down the street on guard, either the county guy's car or the Cliff Shores guy.

He noted the elderly couple went out for a walk on the beach each afternoon, and shortly after they left, the girl would cross the alley and go up the outside stairs to the weird guy's house, where she would stay for an hour or so.

Clearly they had been working together, conspiring against him.

And most important Damian noted that the weird guy sat by the same window much of the day and night, making him an easy target.

And by Thursday, the police were getting sloppy, leaving the area unguarded for close to half an hour as the two officers met down the beach for coffee.

Perhaps Friday would be the day, perhaps Friday the police would be sloppy again, and if they were, Damian would be ready.

That would be the day the weird guy would die, that would be the day the people across the street would pay for putting up that damned *thing* on the roof.

🐦 🐦 🐦

For Kelly Chambers, the week was spent cleaning up company business. Most of the board felt George Johannsen was no longer compatible, and Kelly jumped into the middle of things, arranging a deal whereby the other investors would buy Johannsen out, at a premium but with a promise that the new game title would be on the market within a month, just as school was starting, and it could then be discounted by the holiday shopping season.

Fortunately neither the other board members nor the investors were interested in regular meals with Kelly, so she was able to return to a more-normal diet. She discovered a Del Taco fast-food restaurant just down Mission Street from the San Francisco office, and a halfway-decent hot dog stand by one of the BART mass-transit stations.

Fortunately, too, Kelly was seeing light at the end of the tunnel, that is, a timetable as to when she'd be able to return to New York.

🐦 🐦 🐦

Orland Kramer set the phone down with a note of satisfaction. He had just called the construction crew the city had hired to demolish the rooftop structure, and the job was set for Saturday noontime.

That would make Walker happy. He would get his view back. Kramer wasn't so concerned about that, though.

It was the principle for Kramer.

Though he had grown cynical after too many political battles in previous jobs over the years, and though his post in Cliff Shores had proved no different, somewhere inside Kramer was a dedicated civil servant, one who wanted badly to do a first-rate job.

Leaving the dangerous structure up on that rooftop, in a spot regularly belted by heavy winds, that was not first-rate work, murder or no murder.

And jobwise, as it turned out, Kramer was still likely to be employed a bit longer in Cliff Shores.

When the City Council heard funding for the community center had been diverted, the members blamed the mayor. At a council session Tuesday night Kramer explained his version of what had happened, though sparing the ugly details of Chief O'Brian's hiding in Hawaii, and then promised he would head a new effort to secure funding for the project.

Mayor Dennings sat quietly sulking the entire time. He had not spoken to Kramer all week.

And if Kramer could hold out for another year and a half, his dedication to cities would be turned to the sea—the deep sea, that is, fishing off Monterey for his retirement.

🪰 🪰 🪰

Chief O'Brian meanwhile was making an exit plan of his own. He met twice during the week with Franz Jacobs over getting involved in a spinoff of the modeling technology.

He was also enjoying what might be his final foray in police work—trying to locate a murderer. Researching and making calls to companies that made and sold hang gliding equipment, he had discovered nothing in the way of evidence so far, but had learned a lot and had more calls out.

And during the coming weekend the regular hang gliders of Cliff Shores would return, and they would all have some questions to answer.

Otherwise, O'Brian figured that maybe the whole murder was for the best, something that would set him on a new path in life, one that might facilitate his dream of retiring on Maui.

18

Friday.

Bill Peterson was starving. He was parked just down the street from the Wangs' house, where Limei's grandmother started cooking early in the afternoon, in the process bombarding him with a storm of aromas—garlic, meats, seafood . . .

Sergeant Peterson liked Chinese food, but he had heard really good Chinese food came not from your local delivery guy, not from Safeway or Panda Express, but from the kitchens of regular people like the Wang family.

And sitting in his squad car smelling the mix of sauces and rice wine, thinking about the small chicken Caesar salad that many hours earlier had purported to be lunch, he was inclined to accept the idea.

He looked at his watch, as he had every three or four minutes for the past three quarters of an hour. It wouldn't be long before Dirk Toland would arrive, and as he had done the previous evening, Peterson would drive down to the Beachfront Café and order one of those excellent Danishes they serve to go along with his coffee.

🐾 🐾 🐾

Friday.

Bernard sat next to the window going over a section of "Murder Mystery 2" with Les, the latter playing remotely in a San Francisco coffee shop.

Bernard had made a dinner of two pricey frozen enchiladas on yellow rice, accompanied by nachos with melted cheese and salsa, several pizza rolls, a grilled cheese sandwich, and a large piece of chocolate cream pie with vanilla ice cream on top.

This he chased down with a half bottle of Pepsi.

"Murder Mystery 2" involved a starlet who lived all alone in a small mansion in Malibu, a famous actress who had retired as age stole away the looks that had made her famous.

Les was playing the murderer, Bernard the starlet. Bernard's job in the opening level was to make it as hard as possible for Les to murder him (her). In the second level, Bernard, and possibly others, would become detectives trying to solve the murder.

It is nighttime, the moon is full, the sky is clear.

In the background a coyote howls.

"A coyote in Malibu?" the starlet asks sarcastically.

"I think Chen Li got some of his research wrong," a mysterious voice says from the dark. "I'll make a note of it. It can't be easy creating Malibu from Beijing."

The starlet sits by the window looking out at the sea. She has just finished her dinner.

Suddenly she hears a noise downstairs. It sounds like a window breaking.

Terrified, she hides in a large oak chest in the bedroom.

There she lies motionless, listening intently.

Footsteps make their way up the stairs, then through the main room, and then closer and closer and closer . . . And suddenly there is a hammering on the top of the oak chest itself, first in one corner, next in another.

The hammering stops as suddenly as it started, the footsteps retreat through the main room and down the stairs.

The starlet tries to open the chest but cannot. It is nailed shut.

"Damn," Bernard says.

🎮 🎮 🎮

Friday.

Damian had arrived at the hillside at noon and settled himself on a short wall just down from the Cliffside Condos, having hidden his rifle in the bushes next to him.

He brought a lunch box with cold sandwiches and yogurt, supplies for both lunch and dinner. He added to that a Thermos of tequila and lemon juice, which he began drinking a few hours after lunch, both to keep his mouth from getting dry and to loosen him up for the tasks at hand.

From his vantage point on the wall Damian could look down on Bill Peterson's squad car, through a row of bushes that kept him hidden. And from there he was able also to monitor the alley, the weird guy's house, and the one across the street.

His plan had two parts, as he had been plotting it all week. First he would kill the weird guy (Bernard), then quickly douse the lower floor with lighter fluid and start a fire to burn away evidence of both murders. Then he would run into the house across the street—the house where someone had built that *thing* on the roof—and shoot whoever he could find before torching it, as well.

It wasn't a terrifically complex scheme: It didn't involve landing a motorized hang glider on a high-rise and flying a body around on a rope, but after his previous murder, Damian had come to believe he was all about simplicity.

And tequila and lemon juice.

🐦 🐦 🐦

Friday.

Limei had a quick dinner but spent time afterward at the table with her grandparents, though the three of them sat largely in silence.

The household had been a happy place the past few days, since Bernard had proved her grandfather was not the murderer, but the atmosphere turned sour Friday afternoon as the specter of the pigeon loft's planned demolition the following morning loomed.

Limei's grandfather finally got up and went out back to smoke a cigarette. He walked out about fifteen yards and sat on a large rock where he could look up and see the pigeon loft on the roof.

For years he had dreamed of one day retiring and raising pigeons. There had to be some way, he reflected. If only it weren't for Fatty across the street.

Limei quietly helped her grandmother clear the table and wash the dishes. When the kitchen was clean she excused herself and went to the living room, where she sat silently playing her old Game Boy—the one Bernard had scratched—with headphones on.

Bernard had turned out to be such a good friend, but not about the pigeons. Limei had prodded him to reconsider having the loft torn down, but Bernard insisted it was a danger, and Limei knew it probably was.

She wished there were something she could do for her grandfather.

Having finished his cigarette, Limei's grandfather climbed up through the tiny trap door leading to the roof.

He wanted to spend a little time in the pigeon loft before going to bed. In the morning he planned to go out and not be there when the construction crew came to demolish it.

His throat hurt at the thought.

He tried to reassure himself that someday he would have a pigeon loft, that someday he would be able to raise and train pigeons.

But deep down inside he knew better. Raising pigeons would remain a dream for him.

And looking out to the sea, Limei's grandfather watched the sun set one final time from his cherished loft.

🐦 🐦 🐦

A dark silhouette through the driver's side window showed the outline of a policeman answering a cell phone.

Damian watched from the bushes above.

After only a couple of seconds the figure set the phone down, started the car and pulled off, in, as Damian had predicted, the direction of the Beachfront Café, where Peterson would sit with Captain Toland and drink coffee for a half an hour—just enough time for some serious murder and arson.

🐦 🐦 🐦

"Where were you on the night of the murder?" asks a tall, slender detective in coat and tails—with Bernard's voice.

"I have three people who will testify I was not at the scene of the crime, that I could not have been at the scene of the crime at the time," says a large, burly man decorated by tattoos and body piercings, but with the voice of Lester Argyle.

"Ah, but a hidden video camera right in the room of the murder shows that in fact you were *there, stabbing the victim multiple times."*

"Oh . . . Oops."

But unbeknownst to Bernard the thug has a plan, is not working alone.

Behind Bernard a window breaks with a loud crash.

Downstairs a window breaks with a loud crash.

A hand comes in, unlocks the window, and pulls it open.

Downstairs a hand pulls open the broken window.

The detective looks at the window.

Bernard looks at a laptop on his desk. One of several small video windows on the screen shows a man with a backpack and a rifle climbing in on the lower floor.

"That's it, fellows, he's here," Bernard says.

And with that the brick-and-mortar Bernard the Detective sprang into action.

🐦 🐦 🐦

Having smashed the window Damian knew he had to move swiftly. He hurried through the empty living room, found the inside stairwell, and climbed hurriedly but silently, hoping to surprise the weird guy.

Opening the door at the top he found himself on the house's middle level, and in the dark he fumbled around to find the second flight of stairs, which would no doubt bring him to the top floor, where he would find, shoot, and kill his target.

That stairwell, too, had a door at the top.

It screeched as Damian gradually slid it open, and there across the room stood Bernard, his back to the door.

Training the rifle at Bernard, Damian slowly entered.

Adrenaline rushed through his body. This was the sort of rush Damian had become a murderer for.

The moment of surprise, the moment of terror for the victim, like when Damian had suddenly appeared out of the foggy sky to murder the bird guy.

The moment of shock.

"It's about time you got here," the weird guy said spinning around.

"Wh—, wh—?"

All the planned shock shot right back at Damian.

"I said it's about time you got here, so we can finally get this murder business done with."

Damian squinted. There was just enough light to see Bernard across the room. He appeared to be under some sort of awning, one that seemed to be covered with cloth of some sort.

"You might as well confess," the weird guy said. "I know everything."

"No, no, that's impossible."

Now, Damian had spent weeks planning the bird guy's murder. He had ordered the motorized hang glider from a company in Taiwan, had had it shipped unassembled to a private post office account in San Francisco, and was careful to leave no link of the order and shipping to him.

So how did the weird guy know about it?

On two different nights when the fog was thick, Damian had flown the route from the hills to the Cliffside Condos rooftop and then down to the water. He had memorized the route and all obstacles (that were there then!!!) along the way.

So how did the weird guy know about it?

He then carried out a brilliant murder, one which no one ever would be able to solve.

So how did the weird guy know about it?

"Impossible," he said.

"It is not only possible, it is true," the weird guy responded.

"How could you *possibly* have found out?"

"Well, the police weren't solving the murder, so I had to."

"And you think you're so smart?"

"As a matter of fact, yes, I do. Allow me to introduce myself. I am Bernard Walker."

Keeping the rifle trained on his target, Damian took the opportunity to glance around him at the strange room.

"What the hell is that?" he said looking at the Princess Leia statue.

"That, sir, is Princess Leia. Hasn't anybody in this town seen 'Star Wars'?"

Damian shook his head. "Why doesn't she have any clothes on?"

"Well, you see, a big fat sluglike creature named Jabba the Hutt made her dress that way."

"Are you some kind of pervert?"

"No. And you would be . . .?"

"What?"

"You would be . . . as in your *name?*"

"It's none of your business."

"I assume you are here to kill me," Bernard shot back. "At least let me know the name of the man who is pulling the trigger."

"OK, it's Damian, Damian Mitchell," he said, anger in his voice.

"And why'd you do it?" Bernard asked. "Just to protect your hang gliding? You can hang glide all up and down the coast."

How could he know?

"I chose Cliff Shores. I was here first. That bastard Lowe was trying to ban hang gliding here, where I spent my life's savings to buy a house where I can see the cliffs."

"But murder is rather extreme, isn't it? You could have just moved."

"Not when my home value plummeted forty percent, I couldn't. And you see, that Lowe had also bought the condo he was in—so that he could watch those stupid birds. It was his dream home or mine. I had my home and I had my honor to protect. That Lowe wasn't going to take either away from me."

"Why didn't you just shoot him and be done with it? Why go to all the trouble with a hang glider?"

"Are you kidding? If Lowe was found murdered, I'd be the obvious suspect. I spoke out against his *bird sanctuary* at public meetings. But if he just disappeared, never to be seen again, I'd be home free. It was the perfect crime."

"Did you kill him on the roof, or did he die when he hit the structure across the street?"

How did he know?!

Damian glanced to his right, could just make out the damned thing on the roof through the dark night.

"That damned thing wasn't supposed to be there," he growled.

"Did you kill him on the condo roof?"

"Yes, he deserved it. And now I'm going to kill *you!*"

🐦 🐦 🐦

Along her way to bed Limei noticed the trap door to the roof was still open and she climbed the ladder to find her grandfather there.

She crawled out and sat down next to him.

"We'll find a way to build a new bird loft," she said to him. "Really, we will. I'll make Bernard help somehow. He's a nice guy, really he is."

"Wo zhidao (I know)," her grandfather said. "Ni zao yidian qu shuijiao (You go ahead and go to sleep)."

"No, I want to sit here with you for a few moments."

But before he could respond, the two of them had their attention suddenly drawn away.

🐦 🐦 🐦

Damian pointed the rifle at Bernard's head . . .

He aimed, fit Bernard's nose in the rifle's sight . . .

He squeezed the trigger . . .

And fired, hit Bernard right between the eyes, the bullet ripping a hole the size of a golf ball through Bernard's face.

Or, rather, through the image of Bernard's face on the left-most TV screen, which had been set against the wall and covered with towels, so that it did not appear to be a TV screen.

It was the TV screen that Damian had been talking to.

Bernard himself was sitting in front of a camera in the empty bedroom below, using only the glow of a Zippo for light—a trick he had learned as a Halloween prank when young, making a video on a TV screen look real.

And in the dim light, Damian thought he had been talking to the real Bernard.

Now, there's a thrill some murderers get when killing someone. Damian had experienced it when he killed the bird man, when he swung the large iron flashlight repeatedly at the bird man's head, making a damp thumping noise and with each consecutive bash reshaped the man's skull and face.

And the bird man's head behaved very much the way Damian expected a human head would when smashed with an iron flashlight, getting dented and bloody, the body attached to it getting quieter and stiller.

But Bernard's head was not behaving at all the way Damian expected a human head to behave when shot between the eyes with a hunting rifle.

Bernard's head, rather, seemed to shatter as if made of glass, and worse, it exploded with sparks and smoke in the air around it as though the weird man were a robot.

And before Damian could come to grips with the sight or make any sense of it, three other screens lit up, each one showing Bernard, standing, quite alive, and leering at Damian.

Then the three Bernards spoke at once: "It is not at all polite to shoot people," Bernard said. "In fact it is considered to be terrible manners."

Damian realized now in the added light that he was looking at video screens, though he was completely disoriented by the sight of so many large screens in this strange room.

Stumbling, he shot one of them, creating another plume of smoke and sparks, then became more disoriented as the added light outlined the form of scantily clad Princess Leia.

Shaking his head in disbelief, he aimed the gun and blew Leia's head clean off her shoulders, and was further shocked *not* to see sparks and smoke fly from her.

Damian began turning in a circle, looking at every object, every doorway, every window, his gun half-raised, finger on the trigger . . .

The fifth screen lit, the centermost.

"Watch this," Bernard said on the other two. And the newly lit screen showed a motorized hang glider landing on the roof of the Cliffside Condo building, a roof with surprising detail—telescopes, bird-watching books, the lined tables, and all.

A very recognizable Herbert Lowe turns to face the rider as he lands. The rider walks over to Lowe and begins hitting him repeatedly over the head until the Lowe avatar falls to the ground. The rider then connects a rope to Lowe's foot.

With Damian staring in complete disbelief, the figure jumps onto the rear table, runs down the row, and lifts into the air until the rope is taut and the body lifts . . . and in seconds gains the height needed to clear the safety wall.

The wall cleared, the hang glider rises another five yards for extra power, aims downward slightly, then glides out toward the water.

The view out to the Pacific is clear, it is going to be a clean, easy flight. But off to the north dark letters appear, a sans serif font in a box saying "Nighttime," and the scene changes to night.

Another box flashes, this one with the words "Add marine layer, make it foggy!" and everything goes white.

Then a caption at the bottom: "Ssshhheeeiii****!!!"

The figure is now power hang gliding with only limited visibility.

But it looks right. Lights in the weird guy's house appear where they are supposed to be, so the path to the sea should be clear.

Then suddenly something appears in the way, something that is not supposed to be there—directly in the hang glider's path. Damian looks at it, then just to the right of the screen, at the real thing out the window. *The thing!*

"Ssshhheeeiii—!!!" the brick-and-mortar Damian says not entirely under his breath.

Next the fog disappears and Damian watches as the body hits the rooftop structure and the hang glider and its avatar go careening toward the ocean. Both crash into the water, where the glider sinks under the weight of the motor and the rider avatar is left bobbing up and down—all as the losing horn "Duh, duh, duh . . ." echoes across the sky.

Damian steps back and collapses into a chair. Somehow the weird guy has a high-definition animation of exactly what happened on the night of the murder.

🎮 🎮 🎮

Bernard's plan was working out perfectly. He had called 911 first thing. He knew that with a police car right down the street, help would arrive at any second. By now certainly he had stalled the murderer long enough.

🎮 🎮 🎮

Captain Toland and Sergeant Peterson sat at the Beachfront Café, which had surprisingly little business for a Friday night.

The two of them had been watching Bernard's building in shifts all week.

Toland had just driven back to Cliff Shores from home, and as he did each evening, stopped at the Beachfront Café for a cup of hot coffee before heading over to Bernard's. And tonight, as he had done the previous evening, Peterson went ahead and met Toland at the café, leaving Bernard's house briefly unguarded.

Just as Toland took the first sip of savory hot coffee, his cell phone rang. He answered it to hear a voice reporting a 911 call. A man with a gun was breaking into Bernard's house.

"Shit," Toland said, setting his hot coffee down as he rushed out.

🎮 🎮 🎮

Damian sat staring at the screen in disbelief. How was this possible?

His surprised doubled when another screen lit.

"Dude!" It was Lester Argyle. "You, just, like, totally confessed to murder in front of several cameras."

"I . . . I . . ."

Another screen switched to show Eric Lyle.

"Yeah, guy, you couldn't be any dumber than that, could you?"

Damian jumped to his feet.

"I'm going to kill both of you! Come on, where are you?!" Damian looked around in desperation for doors.

"Dude, you say you're going to kill me and you think I'll tell you where I am?" Lester teased.

"*I'll* tell you where *I* am, guy," Eric said.

"Yeah, where?"

"In the living room."

"I'm coming to get you then! Where's this living room?"

"In Daly City, dude, about an hour away. Want me to leave a light on?"

"Oh, yeah," Lester said, "that's right. You *can't* just come right over and shoot us *because we're not in Cliff Shores.* In fact, I'm all the way up in the Mission District."

Damian's face turned a shade redder as he aimed the gun and shot Lester Argyle right between the eyes, creating a similar explosion of smoke and sparks as shooting Bernard had.

"Dude," Lester continued despite his disappearance from the screen. "I'm still here, and I can still see you. Now, is that Mitchell as in M-I-T-C-H-E-L-L?"

"Rrrrrrr!!!!" Damian screamed and shot out the screen with Eric Lyle on it.

And staring in that direction caught sight of Limei and her grandfather on the structure across the alleyway.

🎮 🎮 🎮

Bernard sat in the dark room watching events on a laptop before him.

Where were the police? They should have arrived by now, should have had the murderer in handcuffs. That irritating Toland always hanging around and giving him dirty looks was the only thing Bernard had come to count on lately.

Bernard tried to think. He'd have to face the murderer himself.

🐔 🐔 🐔

"That was a gunshot," Limei said in terror. "Someone's in Bernard's studio with a gun. We have to call the police."

She could see a dark figure moving about, but couldn't make out a face in the dim light.

A moment later another shot rang out. Limei froze in terror.

And moments later the room lit up with a third shot, then a fourth. There was now just enough light for Limei to see the figure's eyes—staring back at her.

"Quick, we have to run!" Limei shouted, pulling her grandfather down to the trap door with her, and seeing the figure also moving swiftly for a door.

🐔 🐔 🐔

In a flash Damian descended the stairs to the ground floor, where he hurriedly pulled a can of lighter fluid from his backpack.

No furniture had yet been bought for the ground floor, nor drapes, so there was scarce fuel for him to douse. Instead he poured a puddle of lighter fluid in the middle of the living room space and set it aflame with a barbecue lighter.

Once the fire held steady, Damian rushed out the front door to carry out Part 2 of his plan. He figured Bernard had to be in the house somewhere; the fire would get the weird guy.

And if Damian had just confessed to murder, he was going to take out the people across the street who had caused this whole mess.

He dashed across the alley and jerked at the kitchen window. It wouldn't budge and he couldn't see where the latch might be.

So he ran over to the front door, found it locked, and stepped back, then plunged at the doorknob with a front kick—causing a loud thump but not moving the door.

Bernard looked down from the top of the outside stairwell. Having heard Damian run down the stairs, he had crept quietly up into the studio.

He now watched as Damian tried Limei's kitchen window. Bernard had to protect Limei and her grandparents. Looking around he tried desperately to think of something.

On the outside stairwell he was a sitting duck and he would never make it down the inside stairwell in time to help.

He tried to think, then saw the rope and grappling hook hanging on the rail.

Bernard grabbed it, let out about four feet, and swung it in circles. He quickly managed to hoist the hook onto the top of the pigeon coop.

Their modeling had shown the structure would topple with only a slight jolt, and Bernard figured now was the time to take it down —right on top of Damian. Why wait for the construction crew?

Pulling, he got the hook to catch on a stud and with all his might he yanked—but nothing happened.

Down below he saw Damian kicking at the front door.

Bernard pulled again, still nothing, then again and again. In all their modeling, that much tension would have brought the coop plummeting to the ground.

Damian gave up trying to kick the door open and instead aimed his rifle at the doorknob. Bernard saw that at any moment, Damian would have the door open and it would be too late.

In desperation, Bernard tied his end of the rope to the rail and shakily climbed out onto it, butt first, his hands holding the banister. Edging out slightly, he clumsily flopped his torso—and butt—into the air, trying to pound his weight down onto the rope . . . and still the coop would not budge!

Damian stooped, hand on hip, reeling from the pain of the last kick at the door.

It was all going wrong. It was going more wrong than the first murder had. He was going to have to act fast and then run, and run far away from Cliff Shores.

He looked down the beach and saw two police cars emerge from the downtown area, headed in his direction.

Damian glared at the door, leveled his rifle, and aimed at the lock. He squeezed the trigger, once, twice, three times, then kicked and the door flew open, slamming against a wall.

And there, standing helplessly in the living room, were Limei and her grandfather.

Smiling, Damian slowly but deliberately raised the rifle, soaking in the terrified faces staring back at him. He now found himself jolted by the same glorious rush he had experienced when pounding the bird guy's head.

Damian felt his finger squeezing the trigger—then noticed the expressions of utter fear on his targets' faces were directed not at him but beyond and upward.

Damian looked up to see, incredibly, the weird guy apparently humping—humping something invisible—in midair above, his butt pumping up and down wildly.

"What is he doing?"

Up and down, up and down . . . humping what? There was nothing there!

And with a determined squint in his eyes Damian trained the rifle upward at Bernard, covered the trigger, began to squeeze . . .

When from directly above, a loud crack! Damian looked up, immediately saw his view blanketed by something coming, then blackness . . .

As a thundering pile of lumber and construction materials came clobbering down onto him. Then stopped.

Whatever it had been, it stopped. For a brief, brief moment Damian had the notion he had just survived something catastrophic.

And just as sudden, something much heavier crashed painfully, and everything went black.

Bernard looked up from where he had just landed—on top of the heap of boards—and saw the wide-eyed faces of Limei and her grandfather staring back in disbelief.

"Hi," Bernard said weakly, fumbling about his pockets in search of something to eat.

19

Saturday noontime.

Bernard stood at the window of his studio looking at the remnants of the pigeon coop on Limei's roof: the back wall, one side of the coop, and the base, still blocking his perfect view of the Pacific.

It wouldn't be for long, though; a construction crew was due at two to take it down.

It turned out the structure was a lot stronger than he and his designers had figured, a lesson Bernard learned the hard way, he reflected, looking at the cast on his left arm. It turned out that Limei's grandfather was a lot better carpenter than they had thought.

The night before had been a long one. After the fall, Toland arrived and sprang into action, managing to grab the rifle and frisk and handcuff Mitchell, and still have time to get a fire extinguisher from his car and put out the fire in Bernard's empty living room.

It would be some time before Bernard could use the two lower levels of the house, though up till now he hadn't been using them anyway. And he could come and go on the outside stairs and never need to enter the smoked-out lower section of the house.

Once the fire was out, it seemed, about half the country showed up. That included several fire engines, two ambulances, Chief O'Brian, more police, and the city manager—and a reporter who was running around asking questions.

The police and paramedics finally forced Bernard to go to the hospital, where an X-ray proved he had a fractured wrist. It wound up close to two in the morning when Toland drove him back to the house, which Bernard insisted on staying in despite pleas that he find a hotel for the night.

The upper floor was not in much better shape than the lower levels. Glass from the shot-out TV screens covered much of the center of the room and a burning smell from the screens and from downstairs would linger for days.

But Bernard set his lounge up in the back, next to the refrigerator, where he knew he had two pastrami and cheese sandwiches.

Along with the microwave oven, his laptops, and his beloved sleeping bag.

Now, the morning after, everything seemed surreal: the ruins of the pigeon coop, the burning smell, the mess on the alley below. These all were landmarks of the strange, wild turns his life had taken recently: the funding, buying the house, the pigeon coop, the murder, the investigation . . .

Bernard knew it would make a great video game plot, if he could ever come to grips with it.

He looked down at the rubble and was surprised to find Limei making her way up the outside stairs. When she got to the top, she opened the door but remained on the landing.

"Are you OK?" she asked.

"I am alive, if that's what you mean. What's up?"

"Did you break your arm?"

"Yeah. I have to wear this cast for three weeks," he said, holding up his trophy.

"Ooh. That sucks. I had to wear one once on my foot for a month. I hated it."

"I'll survive."

"I want to thank you. My grandparents do, too. You saved our lives."

"That Mitchell was crazy."

"I know. Can you believe it?"

"But it's over now. Things will finally be back to normal."

"I hope I can still come up and play video games with you."

"I shall be very angry if you do not," Bernard said grandly.

"My grandfather's still sad, though."

"Sad?"

"Yeah. They're going to tear down the pigeon coop today," Limei said, her voice breaking.

"I'm sorry, Limei, but the thing's a menace, a danger to everyone who walks down this alley."

"But raising pigeons was his dream."

"I can't see why!" Bernard shot back. "They can't taste very good."

"What?"

"I can't imagine pigeons tasting very good."

"*What?!* He wasn't going to *eat* them!"

"He wasn't? Then what the hell was he going to do with them?"

"He was going to *race* them."

"*Race* them?" Bernard said, taking on a whole new expression.

Epilogue

Saturday morning, four weeks later.

Bernard sat up in the lounge chair to the scent of early morning air, keeping his eyes closed at first.

The smell of the sea and sound of birds along the beach embellished the spectacular—unbroken-by-pigeon-coop—view of beach and ocean in three directions, framed by rocky hills and cliffs to the north and south.

This was why Bernard had gone into business. This was why he founded a company.

About him on boxes were three laptops connecting him to both the real world and to several virtual ones.

All with the sound of waves rolling gently onto the sand, the scent of the ocean tickling his nostrils.

Suddenly a face appeared above him, to his left.

"You sleep all day?" Limei's grandfather asked with a big toothless grin.

Bernard smiled back. "Yeah, I'm going to sleep all day."

"Oooohhh . . ." Lao Wang said as he continued to climb the outside stairs, up the new flight that led to the state-of-the-art pigeon loft Bernard had built for him on the studio's roof.

Moments later Bernard's spectacular view was joined by the sight of pigeons flying circles in precise formation, prodded by a waving red flag in Lao Wang's hand above.

"Pigeon racing," Bernard said, shaking his head. "How cool is that!"

What was cooler, he thought, was that the company paid for the pigeon loft, wrote it off as a research tool for a new title in the OffCide Studios product pipeline: "World Championship Pigeon Racing."

That title, of course, would follow "Murder Mystery 2: The Story of the Strewed Starlet" and "Murder Mystery 3: The Ordeal of the

Ornamental Ornithologist," the latter of which would feature very realistic modeling.

One other title, "Hang Gliding Hunter: The UnDodoing of the Dodo Birds," had been unanimously relegated to a back-burner position in the pipeline, though remained a favorite pre-beta-level pastime among OffCide engineers when they were supposed to be working on the development of priority projects.

With all of that going on, Kelly Chambers, now back in New York, was meeting with investment bankers to discuss plans for an initial public offering that would put OffCide Studios' valuation far above where the Johannsen-led financing had placed it.

Kelly was also negotiating an acquisition of Chen Li's company in Beijing, though the talks were not going well. So she was planning an outright talent grab of Chen Li and his team, set up under a limited company out of Hong Kong.

Bernard also had an unbeatable quality-control expert by the name of Limei, who with her teenage mind saw things very differently than any of the engineers—though only in their twenties, old men by comparison—and who never hesitated to criticize harshly.

More importantly, with the pigeon coop no longer an obstacle either to his ocean view or his love life, Bernard had a third date with Francine Lin planned for this particular evening. He was taking her to what had become their favorite restaurant: MoMo's MiniMart.

Who said video games couldn't solve everything?

🎮 🎮 🎮

A dot appears high in the sky above the cliffs, a dot that quickly grows larger to the eye as the scene zooms in closer and closer.

A second later the dot takes shape, a blade of wings on the top with . . . with a human . . . a human being hanging from it.

A closer zoom shows it to be a man attached by a harness apparatus. He is in a sitting position as—and now it is clear what the shape is—as the hang glider flies down from the hills above Cliff Shores.

The man in the harness is eating a hot dog.

The apparatus includes a cup holder and in it is a large cup labeled "Pepsi."

Zooming back out and to the south the scene shows the hang glider float toward the beach, picking up speed as the wind blows from the cliffs to the open space of sand and water below.

The figure heads around the roof of Bernard's house and slams directly into the makeshift pigeon coop on Limei's roof, but with the wind still driving the hang glider, the coop is lifted into the air with it, now providing a cabin and wind break for the passenger as he continues his flight.

The combination now waivers a brief moment over the beach, floating first up to one side, then down and back up again to the other, gaining more lift and finally rising higher and higher as it continues out to sea.

And the now-winged pigeon coop flies onward over the Pacific, growing ever smaller to the eye, farther and farther, until it is but a tiny dot, disappearing fast onto the distant horizon and setting sun.

*. . . And maybe we'll do in
a squirrel or two,
while we're poisoning pigeons in the park.*

—*Tom Lehrer*

See Tom Lehrer on YouTube

About the Author

John Sailors lives in the San Francisco Bay Area, where, when not writing or doing mindless proofreading, he plays (and loses) video games with his teenage son. (Of course, he lets him win.)

Also by John Sailors:

Hellacious Homeowner: The Saga of Owen Cash Part I, How *NOT* to Buy a House

Welcome to the world of Owen Cash, a man pushed to finally conform with society and pursue his own slice of the Great American Dream: Homeownership. He journeys forth to battle the trials of financial planning (negative amortization—what the hell is that?), house hunting (kids, go slice that family's tires), and mortgage applications (you need an ultrasound of my kidneys?!), all to please family and society and join the ranks of responsible, landed Americans—just at the height of the real estate boom (ka-pow!).

Available on Kindle at Amazon.com.

Visit us at:

www.storycrest.com

www.facebook.com/StoryCrestPress

Try These Books:

Easy Recipes from Scratch

Authors Nicole L'Esperance and her mother, Marie L'Esperance, present an array of family recipes and gourmet dishes, all tested and presented with stunning photographs, in this new cookbook series that shows cooking from scratch doesn't have to be difficult.

- ### Special Dinners for Two

- ### Weeknight Dinners

- ### Best Brunches and Breakfasts

- ### Easy Pumpkin Recipes: There's more to Pumpkins than Pumpkin Pie!

Available at Amazon.com or visit
www.EasyRecipesFromScratch.com